Ancient Texts and the Bible
Book 3 - Easy Reader Edition

In The Beginning...
From Abraham to Israel

Minister 2 Others

Ancient Texts and the Bible
Book 3

In The Beginning... From Abraham to Israel

Easy Reader Edition

In The Beginning... From Abraham to Israel
ISBN 978-1-947751-21-7

Ancient texts compiled for this series:

The Bible
King James Version 1769

The Book of Enoch
An English translation by Dr. Laurence,
Archbishop of Cashel,
Formerly professor of Hebrew at Oxford, 1833

The Book of Jasher
Faithfully translated 1840
From the original Hebrew into English
Published by J.H. Parry & Company 1887

The Book of Jubilees
By R.H. Charles, Oxford: Clarendon Press, 1913

Ancient Texts and the Bible
series include:

Book 1: In The Beginning... From Adam to Noah

Book 2: In The Beginning... From Noah to Abraham

Book 3: In The Beginning... From Abraham to Israel

Book 4: In The Beginning... From Israel to Egypt

Book 5: In The Beginning... From Egypt to Goshen

Book 6: Israel... From Goshen to Sinai

Book 7: Israel... From Sinai to the Tabernacle

Book 8: Israel... Through the Book of Leviticus

Book 9: Israel... Through the Book of Numbers

Book 10: Israel... Through the Book of Joshua

Table of Contents:

Forward

The **Ancient Texts and the Bible** series synchronizes the manuscripts of Enoch, Jasher, and Jubilees into the Bible, making one complete storyline. The books are interwoven using the Torah as the backbone, and the extra-biblical texts as the fleshing out of that backbone.

The third book in the series contains Genesis chapters 18-30, as well as the book of Jasher chapters 18-31, and the book of Jubilees chapters 16-28.

Though the language in the writings have been updated, replacing words like "*thou*" and "*thine*" with words like "*you*" and "*your*", the integrity of the verses remain.

The "*Easy Reader*" edition is for those who just want to read the storyline and enjoy the journey. The stop signs and complex formatting have been removed so one may merely focus upon the story being told.

The *Expanded Edition* of **Ancient Texts and the Bible** was created for the more studious reader. The various manuscripts have the following formatting applied to them in this edition:

the Bible - Regular

THE BOOK OF ENOCH - ALL CAPITALS

the Book of Jasher - Italics

<u>the Book of Jubilees - Underlined</u>

Where one of the extra-biblical texts reiterates the Bible, the phrase is then put in a **bold font**. Where two manuscripts overlap each other exclusive of the Bible, then both fonts are used. For instance, where Jasher and Jubilees intercept, the text is then formatted as *Italics and Underlined.*

The stop sign is another element to the *Expanded Edition* that is not seen in the *Easy Reader*. This image points to contradictions in the content. Printed versions also contain page numbers within the stop sign revealing the page where contradictory information is located, and vice versa. This information was not feasible to place in the e-book versions since the page numbers vary depending on the font size the reader chooses. Following, is an example from each edition:

Easy Reader Edition:

(Genesis 21:20) (...Jasher 21:16...) (Jubilees 17:13...)
And God was with the lad; and he grew, and dwelt in the wilderness a long time, and became an archer.

Expanded Edition:

(Genesis 21:20) (...Jasher 21:16...) (Jubilees 17:13...)
And God was with the lad; and he grew, and dwelt in the wilderness a long time, **and became an archer.**

Whichever you choose, may you ***Enjoy the Journey***!

Prologue

(Jasher 18:11)
In those days all the people of Sodom and Gomorrah, and of the whole five cities, were exceedingly wicked and sinful against the Lord and they provoked the Lord with their abominations, and they strengthened in aging abominably and scornfully before the Lord, and their wickedness and crimes were in those days great before the Lord.

(Jasher 18:12)
And they had in their land a very extensive valley, about half a day's walk, and in it there were fountains of water and a great deal of herbage surrounding the water.

(Jasher 18:13)
And all the people of Sodom and Gomorrah went there four times in the year, with their wives and children and all belonging to them, and they rejoiced there with timbrels and dances.

(Jasher 18:14)
And in the time of rejoicing they would all rise and lay hold of their neighbor's wives, and some, the virgin daughters of their neighbors, and they enjoyed them, and each man saw his wife and daughter in the hands of his neighbor and did not say a word.

(Jasher 18:15)
And they did so from morning to night, and they afterward returned home each man to his house and each woman to her tent; so they always did four times in the year.

(Jasher 18:16)
Also, when a stranger came into their cities and brought goods which he had purchased with a view to dispose of there, the people of these cities would assemble, men, women and children, young and old, and go to the man and take his goods by force, giving a little to each man until there was an end to all the goods of the owner which he had brought into the land.

(Jasher 18:17)
And if the owner of the goods quarreled with them, saying, What is this work which you have done to me, then they would approach to him one by one, and each would show him the little which he took and taunt him, saying, I only took that little which you gave me; and when he heard this from them all, he would arise and go from them in sorrow and bitterness of soul, when they would all arise and go after him, and drive him out of the city with great noise and tumult.

(Jasher 18:18)
And there was a man from the country of Elam who was leisurely going on the road, seated upon his donkey, which carried a fine mantle of divers colors, and the mantle was bound with a cord upon the donkey.

(Jasher 18:19)
And the man was on his journey passing through the street of Sodom when the sun set in the evening, and he remained there in order to abide during the night, but no one would let him into his house; and at that time there was in Sodom a wicked and mischievous man, one skillful to do evil, and his name was Hedad.

(Jasher 18:20)
And he lifted up his eyes and saw the traveler in the street of the city, and he came to him and said, Where do you come

from and where are you going?

(Jasher 18:21)
And the man said to him, I am traveling from Hebron to Elam where I belong, and as I passed the sun set and no one would suffer me to enter his house, though I had bread and water and also straw and provender for my donkey, and am short of nothing.

(Jasher 18:22)
And Hedad answered and said to him, All that you shall want shall be supplied by me, but in the street you shall not abide all night.

(Jasher 18:23)
And Hedad brought him to his house, and he took off the mantle from the donkey with the cord, and brought them to his house, and he gave the donkey straw and provender while the traveler ate and drank in Hedad's house, and he abode there that night.

(Jasher 18:24)
And in the morning the traveler rose up early to continue his journey, when Hedad said to him, Wait, comfort your heart with a morsel of bread and then go, and the man did so; and he remained with him, and they both ate and drank together during the day, when the man rose up to go.

(Jasher 18:25)
And Hedad said to him, Behold now the day is declining, you had better remain all night that your heart may be comforted; and he pressed him so that he tarried there all night, and on the second day he rose up early to go away, when Hedad pressed him, saying, Comfort your heart with a morsel of

bread and then go, and he remained and ate with him also the second day, and then the man rose up to continue his journey.

(Jasher 18:26)
And Hedad said to him, Behold now the day is declining, remain with me to comfort your heart and in the morning rise up early and go your way.

(Jasher 18:27)
And the man would not remain, but rose and saddled his donkey, and while he was saddling his donkey the wife of Hedad said to her husband, Behold this man has remained with us for two days eating and drinking and he has given us nothing, and now shall he go away from us without giving anything? And Hedad said to her, Be silent.

(Jasher 18:28)
And the man saddled his donkey to go, and he asked Hedad to give him the cord and mantle to tie it upon the donkey.

(Jasher 18:29)
And Hedad said to him, What do you say? And he said to him, That you my lord shall give me the cord and the mantle made with divers colors which you concealed with you in your house to take care of it.

(Jasher 18:30)
And Hedad answered the man, saying, This is the interpretation of your dream, the cord which you saw, means that your life will be lengthened out like a cord, and having seen the mantle colored with all sorts of colors, means that you shall have a vineyard in which you will plant trees of all fruits.

(Jasher 18:31)
And the traveler answered, saying, Not so my lord, for I was awake when I gave you the cord and also a mantle woven with different colors, which you took off the donkey to put them by for me; and Hedad answered and said, Surely I have told you the interpretation of your dream and it is a good dream, and this is the interpretation thereof.

(Jasher 18:32)
Now the sons of men give me four pieces of silver, which is my charge for interpreting dreams, and of you only I require three pieces of silver.

(Jasher 18:33)
And the man was provoked at the words of Hedad, and he cried bitterly, and he brought Hedad to Serak judge of Sodom.

(Jasher 18:34)
And the man laid his cause before Serak the judge, when Hedad replied, saying, It is not so, but thus the matter stands; and the judge said to the traveler, This man Hedad tells you truth, for he is famed in the cities for the accurate interpretation of dreams.

(Jasher 18:35)
And the man cried at the word of the judge, and he said, Not so my Lord, for it was in the day that I gave him the cord and mantle which was upon the donkey, in order to put them by in his house; and they both disputed before the judge, the one saying, Thus the matter was, and the other declaring otherwise.

(Jasher 18:36)
And Hedad said to the man, Give me four pieces of silver that

I charge for my interpretations of dreams; I will not make any allowance; and give me the expense of the four meals that you ate in my house.

(Jasher 18:37)
And the man said to Hedad, Truly I will pay you for what I ate in your house, only give me the cord and mantle which you concealed in your house.

(Jasher 18:38)
And Hedad replied before the judge and said to the man, Did I not tell you the interpretation of your dream? The cord means that your days shall be prolonged like a cord, and the mantle, that you will have a vineyard in which you will plant all kinds of fruit trees.

(Jasher 18:39)
This is the proper interpretation of your dream, now give me the four pieces of silver that I require as a compensation, for I will make you no allowance.

(Jasher 18:40)
And the man cried at the words of Hedad and they both quarreled before the judge, and the judge gave orders to his servants, who drove them rashly from the house.

(Jasher 18:41)
And they went away quarreling from the judge, when the people of Sodom heard them, and they gathered about them and they exclaimed against the stranger, and they drove him rashly from the city.

(Jasher 18:42)
And the man continued his journey upon his donkey with

bitterness of soul, lamenting and weeping.

(Jasher 18:43)
And while he was going along he wept at what had happened to him in the corrupt city of Sodom.

Genesis: Chapter Eighteen

(Jasher 18:2)
And in the third day Abraham went out of his tent and sat at the door to enjoy the heat of the sun, during the pain of his flesh.

(Genesis 18:1) (Jasher 18:4...) (Jubilees 16:1...)
And on the new moon of the fourth month the LORD appeared to Abraham in the plains at the oak of Mamre: and sent three of his ministering angels to visit him, and he sat in the tent door in the heat of the day.

(Genesis 18:2) (...Jasher 18:4)
And Abraham lifted up his eyes and looked, and, lo, three men were coming from a distance and they stood by him: and when he saw them, he rose up and ran to meet them from the tent door, and he bowed himself down toward the ground to them and brought them into his house.

(Genesis 18:3) (Jasher 18:5...)
And he said to them, My Lord, if now I have found favor in Your sight, do not pass by, I pray, from Your servant:

(Genesis 18:4)
Let a little water, I pray, be fetched, and wash Your feet, and rest Yourselves under the tree:

(Genesis 18:5) (...Jasher 18:5...)
Turn in and I will fetch a morsel of bread, and comfort Your hearts; after that, You shall pass on: for therefore are You

come to your servant. And he pressed them, and they turned in and they said, Do as you have said.

(...Jasher 18:5)
And he gave them water and they washed their feet, and he placed them under a tree at the door of the tent.

(Genesis 18:6) (Jasher 18:7)
And Abraham hurried into the tent to Sarah, and he said to her, Make ready quickly three measures of fine meal, knead it, and make cakes on the hearth to cover the pot containing the meat, and she did so.

(Genesis 18:7) (Jasher 18:6)
And Abraham ran to the herd, and fetched a calf tender and good, and he hurried to kill it and gave it to a young man, his servant Eliezer; and he hurried to dress it.

(Genesis 18:8) (Jasher 18:8)
And Abraham hurried and he took butter, and milk, and the calf which he had dressed, and mutton and set it before them to eat before the flesh of the calf was sufficiently done, and he stood by them under the tree, and they ate.

(Genesis 18:9)
And they said to him, Where is Sarah your wife? And he said, Behold, in the tent.

(Genesis 18:10) (Jasher 18:9) (...Jubilees 16:1)
And when they had done eating He said to him, I will certainly return to you according to the time of life; and, lo, Sarah your wife shall have a son. And Sarah heard it in the tent door, which was behind him.

(Genesis 18:11)

Now Abraham and Sarah were old and well stricken in age; and it ceased to be with Sarah after the manner of women.

(Genesis 18:12) (Jubilees 16:2....)

Therefore, Sarah laughed within herself, for she heard that we had spoken these words with Abraham, saying, After I am waxed old shall I have pleasure, my lord being old also?

(Genesis 18:13)

And the LORD said to Abraham, Why did Sarah laugh, saying, Shall I of a surety bear a child, which am old?

(Genesis 18:14) (Jubilees 16:4)

Is anything too hard for the LORD? At the time appointed I will return to you, according to the time of life, and Sarah shall have a son.

(Genesis 18:15) (...Jubilees 16:2)

And we admonished her, and Sarah denied that she had laughed on account of the words, saying, I did not laugh; for she was afraid. And He said, Nay; but you did laugh.

(Jubilees 16:3)

And we told her the name of her son, as his name is ordained and written in the heavenly tablets - Isaac.

(Genesis 18:16) (Jasher 18:10)

And afterward the men rose up and departed from there, and looked toward Sodom: and went their ways, to the places to which they were sent and Abraham went with them to bring them on the way.

(Genesis 18:17)
And the LORD said, Shall I hide from Abraham what I am doing;

(Genesis 18:18)
Seeing that Abraham shall surely become a great and mighty nation, and all the nations of the earth shall be blessed in him?

(Genesis 18:19)
For I know him, that he will command his children and his household after him, and they shall keep the way of the LORD, to do justice and judgment; that the LORD may bring on Abraham that which He has spoken of him.

(Genesis 18:20)
And the LORD said, Because the cry of Sodom and Gomorrah is great, and because their sin is very grievous;

(Genesis 18:21)
I will go down now, and see whether they have done altogether according to the cry of it, which is come to Me; and if not, I will know.

(Genesis 18:22)
And the men turned their faces from there, and went toward Sodom: but Abraham stood before the LORD.

(Genesis 18:23)
And Abraham drew near, and said, Will You also destroy the righteous with the wicked?

(Genesis 18:24)
Peradventure there be fifty righteous within the city: will You

also destroy and not spare the place for the fifty righteous that are therein?

(Genesis 18:25)
That be far from You to do after this manner, to slay the righteous with the wicked: and that the righteous should be as the wicked, that be far from You: Shall not the Judge of all the earth do right?

(Genesis 18:26)
And the LORD said, If I find in Sodom fifty righteous within the city, then I will spare all the place for their sakes.

(Genesis 18:27)
And Abraham answered and said, Behold now, I have taken on me to speak to the Lord, which am but dust and ashes:

(Genesis 18:28)
Peradventure there shall lack five of the fifty righteous: will You destroy all the city for lack of five? And He said, If I find there forty and five, I will not destroy it.

(Genesis 18:29)
And he spoke to Him yet again, and said, Peradventure there shall be forty found there. And He said, I will not do it for forty's sake.

(Genesis 18:30)
And he said to Him, Oh let not the Lord be angry, and I will speak: Peradventure there shall thirty be found there. And He said, I will not do it, if I find thirty there.

(Genesis 18:31)
And he said, Behold now, I have taken on me to speak to the

Lord: Peradventure there shall be twenty found there. And He said, I will not destroy it for twenty's sake.

(Genesis 18:32)
And he said, Oh let not the Lord be angry, and I will speak yet but this once: Peradventure ten shall be found there. And He said, I will not destroy it for ten's sake.

(Genesis 18:33)
And the LORD went His way, as soon as He had left communing with Abraham: and Abraham returned to his place.

~ ~ ~

(Jasher 19:1)
And the cities of Sodom had four judges to four cities, and these were their names, Serak in the city of Sodom, Sharkad in Gomorrah, Zabnac in Admah, and Menon in Zeboyim.

(Jasher 19:2)
And Eliezer Abraham's servant applied to them different names, and he converted Serak to Shakra, Sharkad to Shakrura, Zebnac to Kezobim, and Menon to Matzlodin.

(Jasher 19:3)
And by desire of their four judges the people of Sodom and Gomorrah had beds erected in the streets of the cities, and if a man came to these places they laid hold of him and brought him to one of their beds, and by force made him to lie in them.

(Jasher 19:4)
And as he lay down, three men would stand at his head and three at his feet, and measure him by the length of the bed, and if the man was less than the bed these six men would stretch him at each end, and when he cried out to them they would not answer him.

(Jasher 19:5)
And if he was longer than the bed they would draw together the two sides of the bed at each end, until the man had reached the gates of death.

(Jasher 19:6)
And if he continued to cry out to them, they would answer him, saying, Thus shall it be done to a man that comes into our land.

(Jasher 19:7)
And when men heard all these things that the people of the cities of Sodom did, they refrained from coming there.

(Jasher 19:8)
And when a poor man came to their land they would give him silver and gold, and cause a proclamation in the whole city not to give him a morsel of bread to eat, and if the stranger should remain there some days, and die from hunger, not having been able to obtain a morsel of bread, then at his death all the people of the city would come and take their silver and gold which they had given to him.

(Jasher 19:9)
And those that could recognize the silver or gold which they had given him took it back, and at his death they also stripped

him of his garments, and they would fight about them, and he that prevailed over his neighbor took them.

(Jasher 19:10)
They would after that carry him and bury him under some of the shrubs in the deserts; so they did all the days to any one that came to them and died in their land.

(Jasher 19:11)
And in the course of time Sarah sent Eliezer to Sodom, to see Lot and inquire after his welfare.

(Jasher 19:12)
And Eliezer went to Sodom, and he met a man of Sodom fighting with a stranger, and the man of Sodom stripped the poor man of all his clothes and went away.

(Jasher 19:13)
And this poor man cried to Eliezer and supplicated his favor on account of what the man of Sodom had done to him.

(Jasher 19:14)
And he said to him, Why do you act thus to the poor man who came to your land?

(Jasher 19:15)
And the man of Sodom answered Eliezer, saying, Is this man your brother, or have the people of Sodom made you a judge this day, that you speak about this man?

(Jasher 19:16)
And Eliezer strove with the man of Sodom on account of the poor man, and when Eliezer approached to recover the poor

man's clothes from the man of Sodom, he hurried and with a stone smote Eliezer in the forehead.

(Jasher 19:17)
And the blood flowed copiously from Eliezer's forehead, and when the man saw the blood he caught hold of Eliezer, saying, Give me my hire for having rid you of this bad blood that was in your forehead, for such is the custom and the law in our land.

(Jasher 19:18)
And Eliezer said to him, You have wounded me and require me to pay you your hire; and Eliezer would not hearken to the words of the man of Sodom.

(Jasher 19:19)
And the man laid hold of Eliezer and brought him to Shakra the judge of Sodom for judgment.

(Jasher 19:20)
And the man spoke to the judge, saying, I beseech you my lord, thus has this man done, for I smote him with a stone that the blood flowed from his forehead, and he is unwilling to give me my hire.

(Jasher 19:21)
And the judge said to Eliezer, This man speak truth to you, give him his hire, for this is the custom in our land; and Eliezer heard the words of the judge, and he lifted up a stone and smote the judge, and the stone struck on his forehead, and the blood flowed copiously from the forehead of the judge, and Eliezer said, If this then is the custom in your land, give to this man what I should have given him, for this has been your decision, you decreed it.

(Jasher 19:22)
And Eliezer left the man of Sodom with the judge, and he went away.

(Jasher 19:23)
And when the kings of Elam had made war with the kings of Sodom, the kings of Elam captured all the property of Sodom, and they took Lot captive, with his property, and when it was told to Abraham he went and made war with the kings of Elam, and he recovered from their hands all the property of Lot as well as the property of Sodom.

(Jasher 19:24)
At that time the wife of Lot bare him a daughter, and he called her name Paltith, saying, Because God had delivered him and his whole household from the kings of Elam; and Paltith daughter of Lot grew up, and one of the men of Sodom took her for a wife.

(Jasher 19:25)
And a poor man came into the city to seek a maintenance, and he remained in the city some days, and all the people of Sodom caused a proclamation of their custom not to give this man a morsel of bread to eat, until he dropped dead upon the earth, and they did so.

(Jasher 19:26)
And Paltith the daughter of Lot saw this man lying in the streets starved with hunger, and no one would give him anything to keep him alive, and he was just upon the point of death.

(Jasher 19:27)
And her soul was filled with pity on account of the man, and

she fed him secretly with bread for many days, and the soul of this man was revived.

(Jasher 19:28)
For when she went forth to fetch water she would put the bread in the water pitcher, and when she came to the place where the poor man was, she took the bread from the pitcher and gave it him to eat; so she did many days.

(Jasher 19:29)
And all the people of Sodom and Gomorrah wondered how this man could bear starvation for so many days.

(Jasher 19:30)
And they said to each other, This can only be that he eats and drinks, for no man can bear starvation for so many days or live as this man has, without even his countenance changing; and three men concealed themselves in a place where the poor man was stationed, to know who it was that brought him bread to eat.

(Jasher 19:31)
And Paltith daughter of Lot went forth that day to fetch water, and she put bread into her pitcher of water, and she went to draw water by the poor man's place, and she took out the bread from the pitcher and gave it to the poor man and he ate it.

(Jasher 19:32)
And the three men saw what Paltith did to the poor man, and they said to her, It is you then who have supported him, and therefore has he not starved, nor changed in appearance nor died like the rest.

(Jasher 19:33)
And the three men went out of the place in which they were concealed, and they seized Paltith and the bread which was in the poor man's hand.

(Jasher 19:34)
And they took Paltith and brought her before their judges, and they said to them, Thus did she do, and it is she who supplied the poor man with bread, therefore he did not die all this time; now therefore declare to us the punishment due to this woman for having transgressed our law.

(Jasher 19:35)
And the people of Sodom and Gomorrah assembled and kindled a fire in the street of the city, and they took the woman and cast her into the fire and she was burned to ashes.

(Jasher 19:36)
And in the city of Admah there was a woman to whom they did the like.

(Jasher 19:37)
For a traveler came into the city of Admah to abide there all night, with the intention of going home in the morning, and he sat opposite the door of the house of the young woman's father, to remain there, as the sun had set when be had reached that place; and the young woman saw him sitting by the door of the house.

(Jasher 19:38)
And he asked her for a drink of water and she said to him, Who are you? And he said to her, I was this day going on the road, and reached here when the sun set, so I will abide here

all night, and in the morning I will arise early and continue my journey.

(Jasher 19:39)
And the young woman went into the house and fetched the man bread and water to eat and drink.

(Jasher 19:40)
And this affair became known to the people of Admah, and they assembled and brought the young woman before the judges, that they should judge her for this act.

(Jasher 19:41)
And the judge said, The judgment of death must pass upon this woman because she transgressed our law, and this therefore is the decision concerning her.

(Jasher 19:42)
And the people of those cities assembled and brought out the young woman, and anointed her with honey from head to foot, as the judge had decreed, and they placed her before a swarm of bees which were then in their hives, and the bees flew upon her and stung her that her whole body was swelled.

(Jasher 19:43)
And the young woman cried out on account of the bees, but no one took notice of her or pitied her, and her cries ascended to heaven.

(Jasher 19:44)
And the Lord was provoked at this and at all the works of the cities of Sodom, for they had abundance of food, and had tranquility among them, and still would not sustain the poor

and the needy, and in those days their evil doings and sins became great before the Lord.

(Jasher 19:45)
And the Lord sent for two of the angels that had come to Abraham's house, to destroy Sodom and its cities.

Genesis: Chapter Nineteen

(Genesis 19:1) (Jasher 19:46)

And the angels rose up from the door of Abraham's tent, after they had eaten and drunk, and there came two angels to Sodom at even; and Lot sat in the gate of Sodom: and Lot seeing them rose up to meet them; and he bowed himself down with his face toward the ground;

(Genesis 19:2)

And he said, Behold now, my lords, turn in, I pray, into your servant's house, and tarry all night, and wash your feet, and you shall rise up early, and go on your ways. And they said, Nay; but we will abide in the street all night.

(Genesis 19:3) (Jasher 19:47)

And he pressed on them greatly; and they turned in to him, and entered into his house; and he made them a feast, and he gave them victuals and baked unleavened bread, and they ate they abode all night in his house.

(Genesis 19:4)

But before they lay down, the men of the city, even the men of Sodom, compassed the house round, both old and young, all the people from every quarter:

(Genesis 19:5)

And they called to Lot, and said to him, Where are the men which came in to you this night? Bring them out to us, that we may know them.

(Genesis 19:6)
And Lot went out at the door to them, and shut the door after him,

(Genesis 19:7)
And said, I pray, brethren, do not so wickedly.

(Genesis 19:8)
Behold now, I have two daughters which have not known man; let me, I pray, bring them out to you, and do you to them as is good in your eyes: only to these men do nothing; for therefore came they under the shadow of my roof.

(Genesis 19:9)
And they said, Stand back. And they said again, This one fellow came in to sojourn, and he will needs be a judge: now will we deal worse with you, than with them. And they pressed sore on the man, even Lot, and came near to break the door.

(Genesis 19:10)
But the men put forth their hand, and pulled Lot into the house to them, and shut to the door.

(Genesis 19:11)
And they smote the men that were at the door of the house with blindness, both small and great: so that they wearied themselves to find the door.

(Genesis 19:12) (Jasher 19:48...)
And the men said to Lot, Do you have any here besides these? Son in law, and your sons, and your daughters? Arise, go forth, you and whatsoever you have in the city, bring them out of this place lest you be consumed in the iniquity of this city;

(Genesis 19:13) (...Jasher 19:48)

For we will destroy this place, because the cry of them is waxen great before the face of the LORD; and the LORD has sent us to destroy it.

(Genesis 19:14)

And Lot went out, and spoke to his sons in law, which married his daughters, and said, Up, get you out of this place; for the LORD will destroy this city. But he seemed as one that mocked to his sons in law.

(Genesis 19:15)

And when the morning arose, then the angels hurried Lot, saying, Arise, take your wife, and your two daughters, which are here; lest you be consumed in the iniquity of the city.

(Genesis 19:16) (Jasher 19:49)

And while he lingered, the men laid hold on his hand, and on the hand of his wife, and on the hand of his two daughters and all belonging to him; the LORD being merciful to him: and they brought him forth, and set him without the city.

(Genesis 19:17) (Jasher 19:50...)

And it came to pass, when they had brought them forth abroad, that he said to Lot, Escape for your life; look not behind you, neither stay you in all the plain; escape to the mountain, lest you be consumed.

(Genesis 19:18)

And Lot said to them, Oh, not so, my Lord:

(Genesis 19:19)

Behold now, your servant has found grace in your sight, and you have magnified your mercy, which you have showed to me in saving my life; and I cannot escape to the mountain, lest some evil take me, and I die:

(Genesis 19:20)

Behold now, this city is near to flee to, and it is a little one: Oh, let me escape there, (is it not a little one?) And my soul shall live.

(Genesis 19:21)

And he said to him, See, I have accepted you concerning this thing also, that I will not overthrow this city, for the which you have spoken.

(Genesis 19:22)

Hurry, escape there; for I cannot do anything till you get there. Therefore, the name of the city was called Zoar.

(...Jasher 19:50)

And Lot fled and all belonging to him.

(Genesis 19:23)

The sun was risen on the earth when Lot entered into Zoar.

(Genesis 19:24) (Jasher 19:51)

Then the LORD rained on Sodom and on Gomorrah and upon all these cities brimstone and fire from the LORD out of heaven;

(Genesis 19:25) (Jasher 19:52...)

And He overthrew those cities, and all the plain, and all the inhabitants of the cities, and that which grew on the ground.

(Jubilees 16:5)

And in this month the Lord executed his judgments on Sodom,

and Gomorrah, and Zeboim, and all the region of the Jordan, and He burned them with fire and brimstone, and destroyed them until this day, even as I have declared to you all their works, that they are wicked and sinners exceedingly, and that they defile themselves and commit fornication in their flesh, and work uncleanness on the earth.

(Jubilees 16:6)
And, in like manner, God will execute judgment on the places where they have done according to the uncleanness of the Sodomites, like to the judgment of Sodom.

(Jubilees 16:7)
But Lot we saved; for God remembered Abraham, and sent him out from the midst of the overthrow.

(Genesis 19:26) (...Jasher 19:52, 53)
But Ado his wife looked back from behind him, to see the destruction of the cities, for her compassion was moved on account of her daughters who remained in Sodom, for they did not go with her. And when she looked back she became a pillar of salt and it is yet in that place to this day.

(Jasher 19:54)
And the oxen which stood in that place daily licked up the salt to the extremities of their feet, and in the morning, it would spring forth afresh, and they again licked it up to this day.

(Genesis 19:27) (Jasher 19:56...)
And Abraham got up early in the morning to the place where he stood before the LORD: to see what had been done to the cities of Sodom;

(Genesis 19:28) (...Jasher 19:56)

And he looked toward Sodom and Gomorrah, and toward all the land of the plain, and beheld, and, lo, the smoke of the country went up as the smoke of a furnace.

(Genesis 19:29)

And it came to pass, when God destroyed the cities of the plain, that God remembered Abraham, and sent Lot out of the midst of the overthrow, when He overthrew the cities in the which Lot dwelt.

(Genesis 19:30) (Jasher 19:55)

And Lot went up out of Zoar, and dwelt in the mountain, and his two daughters with him; for he feared to dwell in Zoar: and he dwelt in a cave of Adullam, he and his two daughters. And they remained there for some time.

(Genesis 19:31) (Jasher 19:57...)

And Lot and his two daughters remained in the cave. And the firstborn said to the younger, Our father is old, and there is not a man in the earth to come in to us that could raise up seed from us after the manner of all the earth: for they thought that the whole earth was destroyed.

(Genesis 19:32)

Come, let us make our father drink wine, and we will lie with him, that we may preserve seed of our father.

(Genesis 19:33) (...Jasher 19:57...)

And they made their father drink wine that night: and the firstborn went in, and lay with her father; and he perceived not when she lay down, nor when she arose.

(Genesis 19:34)

And it came to pass on the morrow, that the firstborn said to the younger, Behold, I lay last night with my father: let us make him drink wine this night also; and go you in, and lie with him, that we may preserve seed of our father.

(Genesis 19:35) (...Jasher 19:57)

And they made their father drink wine that night also: and the younger arose, and lay with him; and he perceived not when she lay down, nor when she arose.

(Genesis 19:36) (Jasher 19:58...)

And they both lay with their father. Thus, both the daughters of Lot were with child by their father.

(Jubilees 16:8)

And Lot and his daughters committed sin on the earth, such as had not been on the earth since the days of Adam till his time; for the man lay with his daughters.

(Jubilees 16:9)

And, behold, it was commanded and engraved concerning all his seed, on the heavenly tablets, to remove them and root them out, and to execute judgment on them like the judgment of Sodom, and to leave no seed of the man on earth on the day of condemnation.

(Genesis 19:37) (...Jasher 19:58)

And the firstborn bore a son, and called his name Moab: saying, From my father I conceived him; the same is the father of the Moabites to this day.

(Genesis 19:38) (Jasher 19:59)

And the younger, she also bore a son, and called his name

Benammi: the same is the father of the children of Ammon to this day.

(Jasher 19:60)
And after this Lot and his two daughters went away from there, and he dwelt on the other side of the Jordan with his two daughters and their sons, and the sons of Lot grew up, and they went and took themselves wives from the land of Canaan, and they begot children and they were fruitful and multiplied.

Genesis: Chapter Twenty

(Genesis 20:1) (Jasher 20:1...) (Jubilees 16:10)

And at that time, in this month, Abraham moved from Hebron, and journeyed from there, the plain of Mamre, and he went toward the south country, to the land of the Philistines, and dwelt between Kadesh and Shur, and sojourned in the mountains of Gerar.

(...Jasher 20:1)

It was in the twenty-fifth year of Abraham's being in the land of Canaan, and the hundredth year of the life of Abraham, that he came to Gerar in the land of the Philistines.

(Jasher 20:2)

And when they entered the land he said to Sarah his wife, Say that you are my sister, to any one that shall ask you, in order that we may escape the evil of the inhabitants of the land.

(Jasher 20:3...)

And as Abraham was dwelling in the land of the Philistines, the servants of Abimelech, king of the Philistines, saw that Sarah was exceedingly beautiful, and they asked Abraham concerning her.

(Genesis 20:2...) (...Jasher 20:3)

And Abraham said of Sarah his wife, She is my sister:

(Jasher 20:4)

And the servants of Abimelech went to Abimelech, saying, A man from the land of Canaan is come to dwell in the land, and he has a sister that is exceeding fair.

(...Genesis 20:2) (Jasher 20:5)
And Abimelech heard the words of his servants who praised Sarah to him, and Abimelech king of Gerar sent his officers, and took Sarah, and they brought her to the king.

(Jasher 20:6)
And Sarah came to the house of Abimelech, and the king saw that Sarah was beautiful, and she pleased him exceedingly.

(Jasher 20:7)
And he approached her and said to her, What is that man to you with whom you came to our land? And Sarah answered and said He is my brother, and we came from the land of Canaan to dwell wherever we could find a place.

(Jasher 20:8)
And Abimelech said to Sarah, Behold my land is before you, place your brother in any part of this land that pleases you, and it will be our duty to exalt and elevate him above all the people of the land since he is your brother.

(Jasher 20:9)
And Abimelech sent for Abraham, and Abraham came to Abimelech.

(Jasher 20:10)
And Abimelech said to Abraham, Behold I have given orders that you shall be honored as you desire on account of your sister Sarah.

(Jasher 20:11)
And Abraham went forth from the king, and the king's present

followed him.

(Jasher 20:12)
As at evening time, before men lie down to rest, the king was sitting upon his throne, and a deep sleep fell upon him, and he lay upon the throne and slept till morning.

(Genesis 20:3) (Jasher 20:13)
But God came to Abimelech in a dream by night, and he dreamed that an angel of the Lord came to him with a drawn sword in his hand, and the angel stood over Abimelech, and wished to slay him with the sword, and the king was terrified in his dream, and said to the angel, In what have I sinned against you that you come to slay me with your sword? And God said to him, Behold, you are but a dead man, for the woman which you have taken; for she is a man's wife.

(Jasher 20:14...)
And the angel answered and said to Abimelech, Behold you will die on account of the woman which you brought last night to your house, for she is a married woman, the wife of Abraham who came to your house;

(Genesis 20:4)
But Abimelech had not come near her: and he said, Lord, will you slay also a righteous nation?

(Genesis 20:5)
Did he not say to me, She is my sister? And she, even she herself said, He is my brother: in the integrity of my heart and innocence of my hands have I done this.

(Genesis 20:6)
And God said to him in a dream, Yes, I know that you did this

in the integrity of your heart; for I also withheld you from sinning against Me: therefore, I suffered you not to touch her.

(Genesis 20:7) (...Jasher 20:14)

Now therefore, restore his wife to the man; for she is his wife; for he is a prophet, and he shall pray for you, and you shall live: but if you do not restore her, know that you shall surely die, you, and all that are yours.

(Jasher 20:15)

And on that night, there was a great outcry in the land of the Philistines, and the inhabitants of the land saw the figure of a man standing with a drawn sword in his hand, and he smote the inhabitants of the land with the sword, yea he continued to smite them.

(Jasher 20:16)

And the angel of the Lord smote the whole land of the Philistines on that night, and there was a great confusion on that night and on the following morning.

(Jasher 20:17)

And every womb was closed, and all their issues, and the hand of the Lord was upon them on account of Sarah, wife of Abraham, whom Abimelech had taken.

(Genesis 20:8) (Jasher 20:18)

Therefore, Abimelech rose early in the morning, with terror and confusion and with a great dread, and he sent and called all his servants in, and he related his dream to them and told all these things in their ears: and the men were very afraid.

(Jasher 20:19)

And one man standing among the servants of the king

answered the king, saying, O sovereign king, restore this woman to her husband, for he is her husband, for the like happened to the king of Egypt when this man came to Egypt.

(Jasher 20:20)
And he said concerning his wife, She is my sister, for such is his manner of doing when he comes to dwell in the land in which he is a stranger.

(Jasher 20:21)
And Pharaoh sent and took this woman for a wife and the Lord brought upon him grievous plagues until he returned the woman to her husband.

(Jasher 20:22)
Now therefore, O sovereign king, know what happened last night to the whole land, for there was a very great consternation and great pain and lamentation, and we know that it was on account of the woman which you took.

(Jasher 20:23...)
Now, therefore, restore this woman to her husband, lest it should befall us as it did to Pharaoh king of Egypt and his subjects, and that we may not die;

(Genesis 20:9) (...Jasher 20:23, 24)
Then Abimelech hurried and called and had Sarah called for, and she came before him, and he called Abraham, and he came before him. And Abimelech said to him, What have you done to us? And what have I offended you, that you have brought on me and on my kingdom a great sin? What is this work you have been doing in saying you are brother and sister, and I took this woman for a wife? You have done deeds to me that ought not to be done.

(Genesis 20:10)

And Abimelech said to Abraham, What did you see, that you have done this thing?

(Genesis 20:11) (Jasher 20:25...)

And Abraham said, Because I thought, Surely the fear of God is not in this place; and they will slay me for my wife's sake.

(Genesis 20:12)

And yet indeed she is my sister; she is the daughter of my father, but not the daughter of my mother; and she became my wife.

(Genesis 20:13)

And it came to pass, when God caused me to wander from my father's house, that I said to her, This is your kindness which you shall show to me; at every place where we shall come, say of me, He is my brother.

(Genesis 20:14) (...Jasher 20:25)

And Abimelech took sheep, and oxen, and men servants, and women servants, and a thousand pieces of silver, and gave them to Abraham, and restored him Sarah his wife.

(Genesis 20:15) (Jasher 20:26)

And Abimelech said, Behold, my whole land is before you: dwell where it pleases you.

(Genesis 20:16)

And to Sarah he said, Behold, I have given your brother a thousand pieces of silver: behold, he is to you a covering of the eyes, to all that are with you, and with all other: thus, she was reproved.

(Jasher 20:27)
And Abraham and Sarah, his wife, went forth from the king's presence with honor and respect, and they dwelt in the land, even in Gerar.

(Jasher 20:28)
And all the inhabitants of the land of the Philistines and the king's servants were still in pain, through the plague which the angel had inflicted upon them the whole night on account of Sarah.

(Jasher 20:29)
And Abimelech sent for Abraham, saying, Pray now for your servants to the Lord your God, that he may put away this mortality from among us.

(Genesis 20:17) (Jasher 20:30)
So Abraham prayed to God on account of Abimelech and his subjects, and the Lord God heard the prayer of Abraham, and he healed Abimelech, and his wife, and his maidservants; and they bore children.

(Genesis 20:18)
For the LORD had fast closed up all the wombs of the house of Abimelech, because of Sarah Abraham's wife.

Genesis: Chapter Twenty-One

(Jubilees 16:11)
And in the middle of the fifth month he moved from there, and dwelt at the Well of the Oath.

(Genesis 21:1) (Jasher 21:1...) (Jubilees 16:12...)
And it was at that time at the end of a year and four months of Abraham's dwelling in the land of the Philistines in Gerar, in the middle of the sixth month that the LORD God visited Sarah as He had said, and the LORD did to Sarah as He had spoken.

(Genesis 21:2) (...Jasher 21:1) (...Jubilees 16:12,13)
And the Lord remembered her, for Sarah conceived, and bore Abraham a son in his old age, in the third month, and in the middle of the month, at the set time of which the Lord God had spoken to him, on the festival of the first fruits of the harvest, Isaac was born.

(Genesis 21:3) (Jasher 21:2)
And Abraham called the name of his son that was born to him, whom Sarah bore to him, Isaac.

(Genesis 21:4) (Jasher 21:3...) (Jubilees 16:14)
And Abraham circumcised his son Isaac being eight days old, as God had commanded him to do to his seed after him; he was the first that was circumcised according to the covenant which is ordained forever.

(Genesis 21:5) (...Jasher 21:3)

And Abraham was a hundred years old, and Sarah ninety years old, when his son Isaac was born to him.

(Genesis 21:6)

And Sarah said, God has made me to laugh, so that all that hear will laugh with me.

(Genesis 21:7)

And she said, Who would have said to Abraham, that Sarah should have given children suck? For I have born him a son in his old age.

(Jubilees 16:15)

And in the sixth year of the fourth week we came to Abraham, to the Well of the Oath, and we appeared to him as we had told Sarah that we should return to her, and she would have conceived a son.

(Jubilees 16:16)

And we returned in the seventh month, and found Sarah with child before us and we blessed him, and we announced to him all the things which had been decreed concerning him, that he should not die till he should beget six sons more, and he should see them before he died; but in Isaac should his name and seed be called:

(Jubilees 16:17)

And all the seed of his sons should be Gentiles, and be reckoned with the Gentiles; but from the sons of Isaac one should become a holy seed, and should not be reckoned among the Gentiles.

(Jubilees 16:18)
For he should become the portion of the Most High, and all his seed had fallen into the possession of God, that it should be to the Lord a people for His possession above all nations and that it should become a kingdom and priests and a holy nation.

(Jubilees 16:19)
And we went our way, and we announced to Sarah all that we had told him, and they both rejoiced with exceeding great joy.

(Jubilees 16:20)
And he built there an altar to the Lord who had delivered him, and who was making him rejoice in the land of his sojourning, and he celebrated a festival of joy in this month seven days, near the altar which he had built at the Well of the Oath.

(Jubilees 16:21)
And he built booths for himself and for his servants on this festival, and he was the first to celebrate the feast of tabernacles on the earth.

(Jubilees 16:22)
And during these seven days he brought each day to the altar a burnt offering to the Lord, two oxen, two rams, seven sheep, one he-goat, for a sin offering, that he might atone thereby for himself and for his seed.

(Jubilees 16:23)
And, as a thank-offering, seven rams, seven kids, seven sheep, and seven he-goats, and their fruit offerings and their drink offerings; and he burnt all the fat thereof on the altar, a chosen offering to the Lord for a sweet smelling savor.

(Jubilees 16:24)
And morning and evening he burnt fragrant substances, frankincense and galbanum, and stackte, and nard, and myrrh, and spice, and costum; all these seven he offered, crushed, mixed together in equal parts pure.

(Jubilees 16:25)
And he celebrated this feast during seven days, rejoicing with all his heart and with all his soul, he and all those who were in his house, and there was no stranger with him, nor any that was uncircumcised.

(Jubilees 16:26)
And he blessed his Creator who had created him in his generation, for He had created him according to His good pleasure; for He knew and perceived that from him would arise the plant of righteousness for the eternal generations, and from him a holy seed, so that it should become like Him who had made all things.

(Jubilees 16:2)
And he blessed and rejoiced, and he called the name of this festival the festival of the Lord, a joy acceptable to the Most High God.

(Jubilees 16:28)
And we blessed him forever, and all his seed after him throughout all the generations of the earth, because he celebrated this festival in its season, according to the testimony of the heavenly tablets.

(Jubilees 16:29)
For this reason, it is ordained on the heavenly tablets concerning Israel, that they shall celebrate the feast of

tabernacles seven days with joy, in the seventh month, acceptable before the Lord - a statute forever throughout their generations every year.

(Jubilees 16:30)
And to this there is no limit of days; for it is ordained forever regarding Israel that they should celebrate it and dwell in booths, and set wreaths on their heads, and take leafy boughs, and willows from the brook.

(Jubilees 16:31)
And Abraham took branches of palm trees, and the fruit of goodly trees, and every day going around the altar with the branches seven times a day in the morning, he praised and gave thanks to his God for all things in joy.

(Genesis 21:8) (Jasher 21:4) (Jubilees 17:1)
And the child grew, and in the first year of the fifth week Isaac was weaned in this jubilee: and Abraham made a great feast in the third month, the same day that his son Isaac was weaned.

(Jubilees 17:2)
And Ishmael, the son of Hagar, the Egyptian, was before the face of Abraham, his father, in his place, and Abraham rejoiced and blessed God because he had seen his sons and had not died childless.

(Jubilees 17:2)
And he remembered the words which He had spoken to him on the day on which Lot had parted from him, and he rejoiced because the Lord had given him seed on the earth to inherit the earth, and he blessed with all his mouth the Creator of all things.

(Jasher 21:5)
And Shem and Eber and all the great people of the land, and Abimelech king of the Philistines, and his servants, and Phicol, the captain of his host, came to eat and drink and rejoice at the feast which Abraham made upon the day of his son Isaac's being weaned.

(Jasher 21:6)
Also Terah, the father of Abraham, and Nahor his brother, came from Haran, they and all belonging to them, for they greatly rejoiced on hearing that a son had been born to Sarah.

(Jasher 21:7)
And they came to Abraham, and they ate and drank at the feast which Abraham made upon the day of Isaac's being weaned.

(Jasher 21:8)
And Terah and Nahor rejoiced with Abraham, and they remained with him many days in the land of the Philistines.

(Jasher 21:9)
At that time Serug the son of Reu died, in the first year of the birth of Isaac son of Abraham.

(Jasher 21:10)
And all the days of Serug were two hundred and thirty-nine years, and he died.

(Jasher 21:11)
And Ishmael the son of Abraham was grown up in those days; he was fourteen years old when Sarah bare Isaac to Abraham.

(Jasher 21:12)
And God was with Ishmael the son of Abraham, and he grew up, and he learned to use the bow and became an archer.

(Jasher 21:13)
And when Isaac was five years old he was sitting with Ishmael at the door of the tent.

(Jasher 21:14)
And Ishmael came to Isaac and seated himself opposite to him, and he took the bow and drew it and put the arrow in it, and intended to slay Isaac.

(Jasher 21:15...)
And Sarah saw the act which Ishmael desired to do to her son Isaac, and it grieved her exceedingly on account of her son.

(Genesis 21:9)
And Sarah saw the son of Hagar the Egyptian, which she had born to Abraham, mocking.

(Jubilees 17:4...)
And Sarah saw Ishmael playing and dancing, and Abraham rejoicing with great joy, and she became jealous of Ishmael.

(Genesis 21:10) (...Jasher 21:15) (...Jubilees 17:4)
Therefore, she sent for Abraham, and she said to Abraham, Cast out this bondwoman and her son: for the son of this bondwoman shall not be heir with my son, even with Isaac for thus he sought to do to him this day.

(Genesis 21:11) (Jubilees 17:5)
And the thing was very grievous in Abraham's sight because

of his maidservant and because of his son that he should drive them from him.

(Genesis 21:12) (Jubilees 17:6)
And God said to Abraham, Do not let it be grievous in your sight because of the lad, and because of your bondwoman; in all that Sarah has said to you, hearken to her voice and do it; for in Isaac shall your seed be called.

(Genesis 21:13) (Jubilees 17:7)
And also of the son of the bondwoman will I make a nation, because he is your seed.

(Genesis 21:14) (Jasher 21:16...) (Jubilees 17:8, 9...)
And Abraham hearkened to the voice of Sarah, and he rose up early in the morning, and took twelve loaves of bread, and a bottle of water, and gave it to Hagar, putting it on her shoulder, and the child, and sent her away: and she departed with her son, and wandered in the wilderness of Beersheba.

(Genesis 21:15) (...Jubilees 17:9, 10...)
And the water was spent in the bottle, and the child thirsted, and was not able to go on, and fell down. And his mother cast the child under one of the shrubs, an olive tree.

(Genesis 21:16) (...Jubilees 17:10)
And she went, and sat her down over against him a good way off, as it were a bow-shot: for she said, Let me not see the death of the child. And she sat over against him, and lift up her voice, and wept.

(Genesis 21:17) (Jubilees 17:11...)
And God heard the voice of the lad; and the angel of God, one of the holy ones, called to Hagar out of heaven, and said to

her, What ails you, Hagar? Fear not; for God has heard the voice of the lad where he is.

(Genesis 21:18) (...Jubilees 17:11)
God has heard your voice, and has seen the child, Arise, lift up the lad, and hold him in your hand; for I will make him a great nation.

(Genesis 21:19) (Jubilees 17:12)
And she opened her eyes, and God opened her eyes, and she saw a well of water; and she went, and filled the bottle with water, and gave the lad drink and she arose and went towards the wilderness of Paran.

(Genesis 21:20) (...Jasher 21:16...) (Jubilees 17:13...)
And God was with the lad; and he grew, and dwelt in the wilderness a long time, and became an archer.

(Genesis 21:21) (...Jasher 21:16, 17) (...Jubilees 17:13)
And he dwelt in the wilderness of Paran with the inhabitants of the wilderness. And he and his mother afterward went to the land of Egypt, and they dwelt there, and his mother took him a wife for her son out of the land among the daughters of Egypt, and her name was Meribah.

(Jubilees 17:14)
And she bare him a son, and he called his name Nebaioth; for she said, 'The Lord was nigh to me when I called on him.'

(Jasher 21:18)
And the wife of Ishmael conceived and bare four sons and two daughters, and Ishmael and his mother and his wife and children afterward went and returned to the wilderness.

(Jasher 21:19)
And they made themselves tents in the wilderness, in which they dwelt, and they continued to travel and then to rest monthly and yearly.

(Jasher 21:20)
And God gave Ishmael flocks and herds and tents on account of Abraham his father, and the man increased in cattle.

(Jasher 21:21)
And Ishmael dwelt in deserts and in tents, traveling and resting for a long time, and he did not see the face of his father.

(Jasher 21:22)
And in some time after, Abraham said to Sarah his wife, I will go and see my son Ishmael, for I have a desire to see him, for I have not seen him for a long time.

(Jasher 21:23)
And Abraham rode upon one of his camels to the wilderness to seek his son Ishmael, for he heard that he was dwelling in a tent in the wilderness with all belonging to him.

(Jasher 21:24)
And Abraham went to the wilderness, and he reached the tent of Ishmael about noon, and he asked after Ishmael, and he found the wife of Ishmael sitting in the tent with her children, and Ishmael her husband and his mother were not with them.

(Jasher 21:25)
And Abraham asked the wife of Ishmael, saying, Where has Ishmael gone? And she said, He has gone to the field to hunt, and Abraham was still mounted upon the camel, for he would not get off to the ground as he had sworn to his wife Sarah

that he would not get off from the camel.

(Jasher 21:26)
And Abraham said to Ishmael's wife, My daughter, give me a little water that I may drink, for I am fatigued from the journey.

(Jasher 21:27)
And Ishmael's wife answered and said to Abraham, We have neither water nor bread, and she continued sitting in the tent and did not notice Abraham, neither did she ask him who he was.

(Jasher 21:28)
But she was beating her children in the tent, and she was cursing them, and she also cursed her husband Ishmael and reproached him, and Abraham heard the words of Ishmael's wife to her children, and he was very angry and displeased.

(Jasher 21:29)
And Abraham called to the woman to come out to him from the tent, and the woman came and stood opposite to Abraham, for Abraham was still mounted upon the camel.

(Jasher 21:30)
And Abraham said to Ishmael's wife, When your husband Ishmael returns home say these words to him,

(Jasher 21:31)
A very old man from the land of the Philistines came hither to seek you, and thus was his appearance and figure; I did not ask him who he was, and seeing you was not here he spoke to me and said, When Ishmael your husband returns tell him thus this man said, When you come home put away this nail

of the tent which you have placed here, and place another nail in its stead.

(Jasher 21:32)
And Abraham finished his instructions to the woman, and he turned and went off on the camel homeward.

(Jasher 21:33)
And after that Ishmael came from the chase he and his mother, and returned to the tent, and his wife spoke these words to him,

(Jasher 21:34)
A very old man from the land of the Philistines came to seek you, and thus was his appearance and figure; I did not ask him who he was, and seeing you was not at home he said to me, When your husband comes home tell him, thus says the old man, Put away the nail of the tent which you have placed here and place another nail in its stead.

(Jasher 21:35)
And Ishmael heard the words of his wife, and he knew that it was his father, and that his wife did not honor him.

(Jasher 21:36)
And Ishmael understood his father's words that he had spoken to his wife, and Ishmael hearkened to the voice of his father, and Ishmael cast off that woman and she went away.

(Jasher 21:37)
And Ishmael afterward went to the land of Canaan, and he took another wife and he brought her to his tent to the place where he then dwelt.

(Jasher 21:38)
And at the end of three years Abraham said, I will go again and see Ishmael my son, for I have not seen him for a long time.

(Jasher 21:39)
And he rode upon his camel and went to the wilderness, and he reached the tent of Ishmael about noon.

(Jasher 21:40)
And he asked after Ishmael, and his wife came out of the tent and she said, He is not here my lord, for he has gone to hunt in the fields, and to feed the camels, and the woman said to Abraham, Turn in my lord into the tent, and eat a morsel of bread, for your soul must be wearied on account of the journey.

(Jasher 21:41)
And Abraham said to her, I will not stop for I am in haste to continue my journey, but give me a little water to drink, for I have thirst; and the woman hurried and ran into the tent and she brought out water and bread to Abraham, which she placed before him and she urged him to eat, and he ate and drank and his heart was comforted and he blessed his son Ishmael.

(Jasher 21:42)
And he finished his meal and he blessed the Lord, and he said to Ishmael's wife, When Ishmael comes home say these words to him,

(Jasher 21:43)
A very old man from the land of the Philistines came hither and asked after you, and you were not here; and I brought

him out bread and water and he ate and drank and his heart was comforted.

(Jasher 21:44)
And he spoke these words to me: When Ishmael your husband comes home, say to him, The nail of the tent which you have is very good, do not put it away from the tent.

(Jasher 21:45)
And Abraham finished commanding the woman, and he rode off to his home to the land of the Philistines; and when Ishmael came to his tent his wife went forth to meet him with joy and a cheerful heart.

(Jasher 21:46)
And she said to him, An old man came here from the land of the Philistines and thus was his appearance, and he asked after you and you was not here, so I brought out bread and water, and he ate and drank and his heart was comforted.

(Jasher 21:47)
And he spoke these words to me, When Ishmael your husband comes home say to him, The nail of the tent which you have is very good, do not put it

(Jasher 21:48)
And Ishmael knew that it was his father, and that his wife had honored him, and the Lord blessed Ishmael.

~ ~ ~

(Jasher 22:1)
And Ishmael then rose up and took his wife and his children and his cattle and all belonging to him, and he journeyed from there and he went to his father in the land of the Philistines.

(Jasher 22:2)
And Abraham related to Ishmael his son the transaction with the first wife that Ishmael took, according to what she did.

(Jasher 22:3)
And Ishmael and his children dwelt with Abraham many days in that land, and Abraham dwelt in the land of the Philistines a long time.

(Jasher 22:4)
And the days increased and reached twenty-six years, and after that Abraham with his servants and all belonging to him went from the land of the Philistines and removed to a great distance, and they came near to Hebron, and they remained there, and the servants of Abraham dug wells of water, and Abraham and all belonging to him dwelt by the water, and the servants of Abimelech king of the Philistines heard the report that Abraham's servants had dug wells of water in the borders of the land.

(Jasher 22:5)
And they came and quarreled with the servants of Abraham, and they robbed them of the great well which they had dug.

(Genesis 21:22) (Jasher 22:6...)
And it came to pass at that time, that Abimelech king of the Philistines heard of this affair, and he with Phichol the chief captain of his host and twenty of his men came to Abraham and spoke to Abraham concerning his servants, saying, God is

with you in all that you do:

(Genesis 21:23)
Now therefore swear to me here by God that you will not deal falsely with me, nor with my son, nor with my son's son: but according to the kindness that I have done to you, you shall do to me, and to the land wherein you have sojourned.

(Genesis 21:24)
And Abraham said, I will swear.

(Genesis 21:25) (...Jasher 22:6)
And Abraham reproved Abimelech because of a well of water, which Abimelech's servants had violently taken away and robbed him.

(Genesis 21:26) (Jasher 22:7)
And Abimelech said to Abraham, As the Lord lives Who created the whole earth, I do not know who has done this thing: neither did you tell me, neither yet I did not hear of the act which my servants did to your servants until this day.

(Genesis 21:27)
And Abraham took sheep and oxen, and gave them to Abimelech; and both of them made a covenant.

(Genesis 21:28)
And Abraham set seven ewe lambs of the flock by themselves.

(Genesis 21:29)
And Abimelech said to Abraham, What do these seven ewe lambs mean which you have set by themselves?

(Genesis 21:30) (Jasher 22:8)

And he said, For these seven ewe lambs you shall take of my hand, I pray you, that they may be a witness to me, that I dug this well. And Abraham took seven ewe lambs and gave them to Abimelech.

(Genesis 21:31) (Jasher 22:9)

And Abimelech took the seven ewe lambs which Abraham had given to him, for he had also given him cattle and herds in abundance, and Abimelech swore to Abraham concerning the well. Therefore, he called that place Beersheba; because there they swore, both of them.

(Genesis 21:32) (Jasher 22:10)

Thus, they made a covenant at Beersheba: then Abimelech rose up, and Phichol the chief captain of his host and all his men, and they returned into the land of the Philistines, and Abraham and all belonging to him dwelt in Beersheba and he was in that land a long time.

(Genesis 21:33) (Jasher 22:11...)

And Abraham planted a large grove in Beersheba, and called there on the name of the LORD, the everlasting God.

(...Jasher 22:11)

And Abraham made to his grove four gates facing the four sides of the earth, and he planted a vineyard in it, so that if a traveler came to Abraham he entered any gate which was in his road, and remained there and ate and drank and satisfied himself and then departed.

(Jasher 22:12)

For the house of Abraham was always open to the sons of men

that passed and repassed, who came daily to eat and drink in the house of Abraham.

(Jasher 22:13)
And any man who had hunger and came to Abra-ham's house, Abraham would give him bread that he might eat and drink and be satisfied, and any one that came naked to his house he would clothe with garments as he might choose, and give him silver and gold and make known to him the Lord who had created him in the earth; this Abraham did all his life.

(Jasher 22:14)
And Abraham and his children and all belonging to him dwelt in Beersheba, and he pitched his tent as far as Hebron.

(Genesis 21:34)
And Abraham sojourned in the Philistines' land many days.

(Jasher 22:40)
And Isaac the son of Abraham was growing up in those days, and Abraham his father taught him the way of the Lord to know the Lord, and the Lord was with him.

(Jasher 22:41)
And when Isaac was thirty-seven years old, Ishmael his brother was going about with him in the tent.

(Jasher 22:42)
And Ishmael boasted of himself to Isaac, saying, I was thirteen years old when the Lord spoke to my father to circumcise us, and I did according to the word of the Lord which he spoke to my father, and I gave my soul to the Lord, and I did not transgress his word which he commanded my father.

(Jasher 22:43)
And Isaac answered Ishmael, saying, Why do you boast to me about this, about a little bit of your flesh which you took from your body, concerning which the Lord commanded you?

(Jasher 22:44)
As the Lord lives, the God of my father Abraham, if the Lord should say to my father, Take now your son Isaac and bring him up an offering before me, I would not refrain but I would joyfully accede to it.

(Jasher 22:45)
And the Lord heard the word that Isaac spoke to Ishmael, and it seemed good in the sight of the Lord, and he thought to try Abraham in this matter.

(Jasher 22:46) (Jubilees 17:15...)
And it came to pass that the day arrived in the seventh week, in the first year thereof, in the first month in this jubilee, on the twelfth of this month, when the sons of God came and placed themselves before the Lord, and Satan also came with the sons of God before the Lord.

(...Jubilees 17:15)
There were voices in heaven regarding Abraham, that he was faithful in all that He told him, and that he loved the Lord, and that in every affliction he was faithful.

(Jasher 22:47)
And the Lord said to Satan, Where do you come from? And Satan answered the Lord and said, From going to and fro in the earth, and from walking up and down in it.

(Jasher 22:48)
And the Lord said to Satan, What is your word to me concerning all the children of the earth? And Satan answered the Lord and said, I have seen all the children of the earth who serve you and remember you when they require anything from you.

(Jasher 22:49)
And when you give them the thing which they require from you, they sit at their ease, and forsake you and they remember you no more.

(Jasher 22:50)
Have you seen Abraham the son of Terah, who at first had no children, and he served you and erected altars to you wherever he came, and he brought up offerings upon them, and he proclaimed your name continually to all the children of the earth.

(Jasher 22:51)
And now that his son Isaac is born to him, he has forsaken you, he has made a great feast for all the inhabitants of the land, and the Lord he has forgotten.

(Jasher 22:52)
For amidst all that he has done he brought you no offering; neither burnt offering nor peace offering, neither ox, lamb nor goat of all that he killed on the day that his son was weaned.

(Jasher 22:53)
Even from the time of his son's birth till now, being thirty-seven years, he built no altar before you, nor brought any offering to you, for he saw that you gave what he requested before you, and he therefore forsook you.

(Jasher 22:54)
And the Lord said to Satan, Have you thus considered my servant Abraham? For there is none like him upon earth, a perfect and an upright man before Me, one that fears God and avoids evil; as I live, were I to say to him, Bring up Isaac your son before Me, he would not withhold him from Me, much more if I told him to bring up a burnt offering before Me from his flock or herds.

(Jasher 22:55) (Jubilees 17:16)
And the prince Mastêmâ, Satan, came before God and answered the Lord and said, Speak then now to Abraham as You have said, behold, Abraham loves Isaac his son, and he delights in him above all things else; bid him offer him as a burnt-offering on the altar, and you will see whether he will not this day transgress and cast aside Your words or if he will do this command, and You will know if he is faithful in everything wherein You do try him.

(Jubilees 17:17)
And the Lord knew that Abraham was faithful in all his afflictions; for He had tried him through his country and with famine, and had tried him with the wealth of kings, and had tried him again through his wife, when she was torn (from him), and with circumcision; and had tried him through Ishmael and Hagar, his maid servant, when he sent them away.

(Jubilees 17:18)
And in everything wherein He had tried him, he was found faithful, and his soul was not impatient, and he was not slow to act; for he was faithful and a lover of the Lord.

Genesis: Chapter Twenty-Two

(Genesis 22:1) (Jasher 23:1) (Jubilees 18:1)
And it came to pass after these things, that God tested Abraham. At that time the word of the Lord came to Abraham, and God said to him, Abraham, Abraham: and he said, Behold, here I am.

(Genesis 22:2) (Jasher 23:2) (Jubilees 18:2)
And He said to him, Take now your beloved son, your only son Isaac, whom you love, and get to the high country, to the land of Moriah; and offer him there for a burnt offering on one of the mountains which I will tell you of, for there will you see a cloud and the glory of the Lord.

(Jasher 23:3)
And Abraham said within himself, How shall I separate my son Isaac from Sarah his mother, in order to bring him up for a burnt offering before the Lord?

(Jasher 23:4)
And Abraham came into the tent, and he sat before Sarah his wife, and he spoke these words to her,

(Jasher 23:5)
My son Isaac is grown up and he has not for some time studied the service of his God, now tomorrow I will go and bring him to Shem, and Eber his son, and there he will learn the ways of the Lord, for they will teach him to know the Lord as well as to know that when he prays continually before the Lord, he will answer him, therefore there he will know the way of serving the Lord his God.

(Jasher 23:6)
And Sarah said, You have spoken well, go my lord and do to him as you have said, but remove him not at a great distance from me, neither let him remain there too long, for my soul is bound within his soul.

(Jasher 23:7)
And Abraham said to Sarah, My daughter, let us pray to the Lord our God that he may do good with us.

(Jasher 23:8)
And Sarah took her son Isaac and he abode all that night with her, and she kissed and embraced him, and gave him instructions till morning.

(Jasher 23:9)
And she said to him, O my son, how can my soul separate itself from you? And she still kissed him and embraced him, and she gave Abraham instructions concerning him.

(Jasher 23:10)
And Sarah said to Abraham, O my lord, I pray you take heed of your son, and place your eyes over him, for I have no other son nor daughter but him.

(Jasher 23:11)
O forsake him not. If he be hungry give him bread, and if he be thirsty give him water to drink; do not let him go on foot, neither let him sit in the sun.

(Jasher 23:12)
Neither let him go by himself in the road, neither force him from whatever he may desire, but do to him as he may say to you.

(Jasher 23:13)
And Sarah wept bitterly the whole night on account of Isaac, and she gave him instructions till morning.

(Jasher 23:14)
Sarah selected a very fine and beautiful garment from those garments which she had in the house, that Abimelech had given to her.

(Jasher 23:15...)
And she dressed Isaac her son therewith, and she put a turban upon his head, and she enclosed a precious stone in the top of the turban, and she gave them provision for the road,

(Genesis 22:3...) (...Jasher 23:15) (Jubilees 18:3...)
And Abraham rose up early in the morning, and saddled his donkey, and took two of his young men with him, and Isaac his son, and clave the wood for the burnt offering, and rose up, and they went forth, and Isaac went with his father Abraham, and some of their servants accompanied them to see them off the road.

(Jasher 23:16)
And Sarah went out with them, and she accompanied them upon the road to see them off, and they said to her, Return to the tent.

(Jasher 23:17)
And when Sarah heard the words of her son Isaac she wept bitterly, and Abraham her husband wept with her, and their son wept with them a great weeping; also those who went with them wept greatly.

(Jasher 23:18)
And Sarah caught hold of her son Isaac, and she held him in her arms, and she embraced him and continued to weep with him, and Sarah said, Who knows if after this day I shall ever see you again?

(Jasher 23:19)
And they still wept together, Abraham, Sarah and Isaac, and all those that accompanied them on the road wept with them, and Sarah afterward turned away from her son, weeping bitterly, and all her men servants and maid servants returned with her to the tent.

(Jasher 23:20)
And Abraham went with Isaac his son to bring him up as an offering before the Lord, as He had commanded him.

(Jasher 23:21)
And Abraham took two of his young men with him, Ishmael the son of Hagar and Eliezer his servant, and they went together with them, and while they were walking in the road the young men spoke these words to themselves,

(Jasher 23:22)
And Ishmael said to Eliezer, Now my father Abraham is going with Isaac to bring him up for a burnt offering to the Lord, as He commanded him.

(Jasher 23:23)
Now when he returns he will give to me all that he possesses, to inherit after him, for I am his first born.

(Jasher 23:24)
And Eliezer answered Ishmael and said, Surely Abraham cast

you away with your mother, and swear that you should not inherit any thing of all he possesses, and to whom will he give all that he has, with all his treasures, but to me his servant, who has been faithful in his house, who has served him night and day, and has done all that he desired me? To me will he bequeath at his death all that he possesses.

(Jasher 23:25)
And while Abraham was proceeding with his son Isaac along the road, Satan came and appeared to Abraham in the figure of a very aged man, humble and of contrite spirit, and he approached Abraham and said to him, Are you silly or brutish, that you go to do this thing this day to your only son?

(Jasher 23:26)
For God gave you a son in your latter days, in your old age, and will you go and slaughter him this day because he committed no violence, and will you cause the soul of your only son to perish from the earth?

(Jasher 23:27)
Do you not know and understand that this thing cannot be from the Lord? For the Lord cannot do to man such evil upon earth to say to him, Go slaughter your child.

(Jasher 23:28)
And Abraham heard this and knew that it was the word of Satan who endeavored to draw him aside from the way of the Lord, but Abraham would not hearken to the voice of Satan, and Abraham rebuked him so that he went away.

(Jasher 23:29)
And Satan returned and came to Isaac; and he appeared to Isaac in the figure of a young man comely and well favored.

(Jasher 23:30)
And he approached Isaac and said to him, Do you not know and understand that your old silly father brings you to the slaughter this day for naught?

(Jasher 23:31)
Now therefore, my son, do not listen nor attend to him, for he is a silly old man, and let not your precious soul and beautiful figure be lost from the earth.

(Jasher 23:32)
And Isaac heard this, and said to Abraham, Have you heard, my father, that which this man has spoken? Even thus has he spoken.

(Jasher 23:33)
And Abraham answered his son Isaac and said to him, Take heed of him and do not listen to his words, nor attend to him, for he is Satan, endeavoring to draw us aside this day from the commands of God.

(Jasher 23:34)
And Abraham still rebuked Satan, and Satan went from them, and seeing he could not prevail over them he hid himself from them, and he went and passed before them in the road; and he transformed himself to a large brook of water in the road, and Abraham and Isaac and his two young men reached that place, and they saw a brook large and powerful as the mighty waters.

(Jasher 23:35)
And they entered the brook and passed through it, and the waters at first reached their legs.

(Jasher 23:36)
And they went deeper in the brook and the waters reached up to their necks, and they were all terrified on account of the water; and while they were going over the brook Abraham recognized that place, and he knew that there was no water there before.

(Jasher 23:37)
And Abraham said to his son Isaac, I know this place in which there was no brook nor water, now therefore it is this Satan who does all this to us, to draw us aside this day from the commands of God.

(Jasher 23:38)
And Abraham rebuked him and said to him, The Lord rebuke you, O Satan, begone from us for we go by the commands of God.

(Jasher 23:39)
And Satan was terrified at the voice of Abraham, and he went away from them, and the place again became dry land as it was at first.

(...Genesis 22:3) (Jasher 23:40) (...Jubilees 18:3...)
And Abraham went with Isaac toward the place that God had told him.

(Genesis 22:4) (Jasher 23:41) (...Jubilees 18:3)
Then on the third day Abraham lifted up his eyes, and saw the place afar off which God had told him of.

(Jubilees 18:4...)
And he came to a well of water.

(Jasher 23:42)
And a pillar of fire appeared to him that reached from the earth to heaven, and a cloud of glory upon the mountain, and the glory of the Lord was seen in the cloud.

(Jasher 23:43)
And Abraham said to Isaac, My son, do you see in that mountain, which we perceive at a distance, that which I see upon it?

(Jasher 23:44)
And Isaac answered and said to his father, I see and lo a pillar of fire and a cloud, and the glory of the Lord is seen upon the cloud.

(Jasher 23:45)
And Abraham knew that his son Isaac was accepted before the Lord for a burnt offering.

(Jasher 23:46)
And Abraham said to Eliezer and to Ishmael his son, Do you also see that which we see upon the mountain which is at a distance?

(Genesis 22:5) (Jasher 23:47) (Jubilees 18:4)
And they answered and said, We see nothing more than like the other mountains of the earth. And Abraham knew that they were not accepted before the Lord to go with them. And Abraham said to his young men, You abide here with the donkey; and I and the lad, Isaac my son, will go yonder and worship, there before the Lord and when we have worshipped then we shall come again to you.

(Jasher 23:48)
And Eliezer and Ishmael remained in that place, as Abraham had commanded.

(Genesis 22:6) (Jasher 23:49) (Jubilees 18:5)
And Abraham took the wood of the burnt offering, and laid it on Isaac his son; and he took the fire in his hand, and a knife; and they went both of them together to that place.

(Genesis 22:7) (Jasher 23:50) (Jubilees 18:6)
And when they were going along, Isaac spoke to Abraham his father, and said, My father: and he said, Here am I, my son. And he said, Behold I see the fire, and the knife, and the wood: but where is the lamb for a burnt offering, father?

(Genesis 22:8...) (Jasher 23:51) (Jubilees 18:7...)
And Abraham answered his son Isaac, My son, God will provide Himself a lamb for a burnt offering: He has made choice of you my son, to be a perfect burnt offering instead of the lamb;

(Jasher 23:52)
And Isaac said to his father, I will do all that the Lord spoke to you with joy and cheerfulness of heart.

(Jasher 23:53)
And Abraham again said to Isaac his son, Is there in your heart any thought or counsel concerning this, which is not proper? Tell me my son, I pray you, O my son conceal it not from me.

(Jasher 23:54)
And Isaac answered his father Abraham and said to him, O my father, as the Lord lives and as your soul lives, there is

nothing in my heart to cause me to deviate either to the right or to the left from the word that he has spoken to you.

(Jasher 23:55)
Neither limb nor muscle has moved or stirred at this, nor is there in my heart any thought or evil counsel concerning this.

(Jasher 23:56)
But I am of joyful and cheerful heart in this matter, and I say, Blessed is the Lord who has this day chosen me to be a burnt offering before Him.

(...Genesis 22:8) (Jasher 23:57)
And Abraham greatly rejoiced at the words of Isaac, and they went both of them and came together to that place that the Lord had spoken of.

(Genesis 22:9...) (Jasher 23:58, 59) (...Jubilees 18:7, 8...)
And they came to the place of the mount of God which God had told him of; and Abraham approached to build an altar there, and Abraham was weeping, and Isaac took stones and mortar until they had finished building the altar. And Abraham took the wood and laid the wood in order, upon the altar which he had built.

(...Genesis 22:9...) (Jasher 23:60) (...Jubilees 18: 8...)
And he took and bound Isaac his son, in order to place him upon the wood which was upon the altar, to slay him for a burnt offering before the Lord.

(Jasher 23:61)
And Isaac said to his father, Bind me securely and then place me upon the altar lest I should turn and move, and break loose from the force of the knife upon my flesh and thereof

profane the burnt offering; and Abraham did so.

(Jasher 23:62)
And Isaac still said to his father, O my father, when you shall have slain me and burnt me for an offering, take with you that which shall remain of my ashes to bring to Sarah my mother, and say to her, This is the sweet smelling savor of Isaac; but do not tell her this if she should sit near a well or upon any high place, lest she should cast her soul after me and die.

(Jasher 23:63)
And Abraham heard the words of Isaac, and he lifted up his voice and wept when Isaac spoke these words; and Abraham's tears gushed down upon Isaac his son, and Isaac wept bitterly, and he said to his father, Hurry, O my father, and do with me the will of the Lord our God as He has commanded you.

(Jasher 23:64)
And the hearts of Abraham and Isaac rejoiced at this thing which the Lord had commanded them; but the eye wept bitterly while the heart rejoiced.

(...Genesis 22:9) (Jasher 23:65...) (...Jubilees 18: 8...)
And Abraham bound his son Isaac, and laid him on the altar on the wood, and Isaac stretched forth his neck upon the altar before his father.

(Genesis 22:10) (...Jasher 23:65) (...Jubilees 18: 8)
And Abraham stretched forth his hand, and took the knife to slay Isaac his son as a burnt offering before the Lord.

(Jasher 23:66)
At that time, the angels of mercy came before the Lord and spoke to him concerning Isaac, saying,

(Jasher 23:67)
O Lord, You are a merciful and compassionate King over all that You have created in heaven and in earth, and You support them all; give therefore ransom and redemption instead of Your servant Isaac, and pity and have compassion upon Abraham and Isaac his son, who are this day performing Your commands.

(Jasher 23:68)
Have You seen, O Lord, how Isaac the son of Abraham Your servant is bound down to the slaughter like an animal? Now therefore let your pity be roused for them, O Lord.

(Jubilees 18: 9)
And I stood before him, and before the prince Mastêmâ, and the Lord said, Bid him not to lay his hand on the lad, nor to do anything to him, for I have shown that he fears the Lord.

(Genesis 22:11) (Jasher 23:69...) (Jubilees 18:10)
At that time, the Lord appeared to Abraham. And the angel of the LORD called to him out of heaven, and said to him, Abraham, Abraham: and he was terrified and he said, Behold, Here am I.

(Genesis 22:12) (...Jasher 23:69) (Jubilees 18:11)
And He said to him, Do not lay your hand on the lad, neither do anything to him: for now I know that you fear the Lord God, in performing this act, seeing you have not withheld your son, your only first-born son from Me.

(Jubilees 18:12...)
And the prince Mastêmâ was put to shame;

(Genesis 22:13) (Jasher 23:70) (...Jubilees 18:12...)
And Abraham lifted up his eyes, and looked, and behold behind him a ram caught in a thicket by his horns: that was the ram which the Lord God had created in the earth in the day that he made earth and heaven.

(Jasher 23:71)
For the Lord had prepared this ram from that day, to be a burnt offering instead of Isaac.

(Jasher 23:72)
And this ram was advancing to Abraham when Satan caught hold of him and entangled his horns in the thicket, that he might not advance to Abraham, in order that Abraham might slay his son.

(Genesis 22:13) (Jasher 23:73) (...Jubilees 18:12)
And Abraham seeing the ram advancing to him and Satan withholding him, went and fetched him and brought him before the altar, and he loosened his son Isaac from his binding, and took the ram, and he put the ram in his stead, and Abraham killed the ram upon the altar, and offered him up for a burnt offering in the stead of his son Isaac.

(Jasher 23:74)
And Abraham sprinkled some of the blood of the ram upon the altar, and he exclaimed and said, This is in the place of my son, and may this be considered this day as the blood of my son before the Lord.

(Jasher 23:75)
And all that Abraham did on this occasion by the altar, he would exclaim and say, This is in the room of my son, and may it this day be considered before the Lord in the place of

my son; and Abraham finished the whole of the service by the altar, and the service was accepted before the Lord, and was accounted as if it had been Isaac; and the Lord blessed Abraham and his seed on that day.

(Genesis 22:14) (Jubilees 18:13)
And Abraham called the name of that place Jehovah Jireh, 'The Lord has seen': as it is said to this day, In the mountain of the LORD it shall be seen: that is Mount Sion.

(Genesis 22:15) (Jubilees 18:14)
And the angel of the LORD called to Abraham out of heaven the second time, as he caused the angels to appear to speak to him in the name of the Lord.

(Genesis 22:16) (Jubilees 18:15...)
And he said, By Myself I have sworn, says the LORD, because you have done this thing, and have not withheld your son, your beloved only son from Me:

(Genesis 22:17) (...Jubilees 18:15...)
That in blessing I will bless you, and in multiplying I will multiply your seed as the stars of the heaven, and as the sand which is on the sea shore; and your seed shall possess the gates and inherit the cities of his enemies.

(Genesis 22:18) (...Jubilees 18:16)
And in your seed, all the nations of the earth shall be blessed; because you have obeyed My voice. And I have shown to all that you are faithful to Me in all that I have said to you: Go in peace.

(Jasher 23:76)
And Satan went to Sarah, and he appeared to her in the figure

of an old man very humble and meek, and Abraham was yet engaged in the burnt offering before the Lord.

(Jasher 23:77)
And he said to her, Do you not know all the work that Abraham has made with your only son this day? For he took Isaac and built an altar, and killed him, and brought him up as a sacrifice upon the altar, and Isaac cried and wept before his father, but he looked not at him, neither did he have compassion over him.

(Jasher 23:78)
And Satan repeated these words, and he went away from her, and Sarah heard all the words of Satan, and she imagined him to be an old man from among the sons of men who had been with her son, and had come and told her these things.

(Jasher 23:79)
And Sarah lifted up her voice and wept and cried out bitterly on account of her son; and she threw herself upon the ground and she cast dust upon her head, and she said, O my son, Isaac my son, O that I had this day died instead of you. And she continued to weep and said, It grieves me for you, O my son, my son Isaac, O that I had died this day in your stead.

(Jasher 23:80)
And she still continued to weep, and said, It grieves me for you after that I have reared you and have brought you up; now my joy is turned into mourning over you, I that had a longing for you, and cried and prayed to God till I bare you at ninety years old; and now have you served this day for the knife and the fire, to be made an offering.

(Jasher 23:81)
But I console myself with you, my son, in its being the word

of the Lord, for you performed the command of your God; for who can transgress the word of our God, in whose hands is the soul of every living creature?

(Jasher 23:82)
You are just, O Lord our God, for all your works are good and righteous; for I also am rejoiced with your word which you commanded, and while my eye weeps bitterly my heart rejoices.

(Jasher 23:83)
And Sarah laid her head upon the bosom of one of her handmaids, and she became as still as a stone.

(Jasher 23:84)
She afterward rose up and went about making inquiries till she came to Hebron, and she inquired of all those whom she met walking in the road, and no one could tell her what had happened to her son.

(Jasher 23:85)
And she came with her maid servants and men servants to Kireath-arba, which is Hebron, and she asked concerning her Son, and she remained there while she sent some of her servants to seek where Abraham had gone with Isaac; they went to seek him in the house of Shem and Eber, and they could not find him, and they sought throughout the land and he was not there.

(Jasher 23:86)
And behold, Satan came to Sarah in the shape of an old man, and he came and stood before her, and he said to her, I spoke falsely to you, for Abraham did not kill his son and he is not dead; and when she heard the word her joy was so exceedingly

violent on account of her son, that her soul went out through joy; she died and was gathered to her people.

(Genesis 22:19...) (Jasher 23:87) (Jubilees 18:17...)
So when Abraham had finished his service he returned with his son Isaac to his young men, and they rose up and went together to Beersheba and they came home;

(Jasher 23:88)
And Abraham sought for Sarah, and could not find her, and he made inquiries concerning her, and they said to him, She went as far as Hebron to seek you both where you had gone, for thus was she informed.

(Jasher 23:89)
And Abraham and Isaac went to her to Hebron, and when they found that she was dead they lifted up their voices and wept bitterly over her; and Isaac fell upon his mother's face and wept over her, and he said, O my mother, my mother, how have you left me, and where have you gone? O how, how have you left me!

(Jasher 23:90)
And Abraham and Isaac wept greatly and all their servants wept with them on account of Sarah, and they mourned over her a great and heavy mourning.

(...Genesis 22:19) (...Jubilees 18:17)
And Abraham dwelt at Beersheba, by the Well of the Oath.

(Jubilees 18:18)
And he celebrated this festival every year, seven days with joy, and he called it the festival of the Lord according to the seven days during which he went and returned in peace.

(Jubilees 18:19)
And accordingly has it been ordained and written on the heavenly tablets regarding Israel and its seed that they should observe this festival seven days with the joy of festival.

(Jasher 22:15)
And Abraham's brother Nahor and his father and all belonging to them dwelt in Haran, for they did not come with Abraham to the land of Canaan.

(Genesis 22:20) (Jasher 22:16)
And it came to pass after these things, that it was told Abraham, saying, Behold, Milcah, the daughter of Haran, and sister to Sarah, Abraham's wife, she has also bore children to your brother Nahor;

(Genesis 22:21) (Jasher 22:17...)
And these are the names of those that were born to him, Huz his firstborn, and Buz his brother, and Kemuel the father of Aram,

(Genesis 22:22) (...Jasher 22:17)
And Chesed, and Hazo, and Pildash, and Jidlaph, and Bethuel, being eight sons, these are the children of Milca which she bare to Nahor, Abraham's brother.

(Genesis 22:23) (Jasher 22:26)
And Bethuel begot Sechar, Laban and their sister Rebekah: these eight Milcah bore to Nahor, Abraham's brother.

(Genesis 22:24) (Jasher 22:18)
And his concubine, whose name was Reumah, she bore also to Nahor: Tebah, and Gaham, and Thahash, and Maachah, being four sons.

(Jasher 22:19)
And the children that were born to Nahor were twelve sons besides his daughters, and they also had children born to them in Haran.

(Jasher 22:20)
And the children of Uz the first born of Nahor were Abi, Cheref, Gadin, Melus, and Deborah their sister.

(Jasher 22:21)
And the sons of Buz were Berachel, Naamath, Sheva, and Madonu.

(Jasher 22:22)
And the sons of Kemuel were Aram and Rechob.

(Jasher 22:23)
And the sons of Kesed were Anamlech, Meshai, Benon and Yifi; and the sons of Chazo were Pildash, Mechi and Opher.

(Jasher 22:24)
And the sons of Pildash were Arud, Chamum, Mered and Moloch.

(Jasher 22:25)
And the sons of Tidlaf were Mushan, Cushan and Mutzi.

(Jasher 22:27)
These are the families of the children of Nahor, that were born to them in Haran; and Aram the son of Kemuel and Rechob his brother went away from Haran, and they found a valley in the land by the river Euphrates.

(Jasher 22:28)
And they built a city there, and they called the name of the city after the name of Pethor the son of Aram, that is Aram Naherayim to this day.

(Jasher 22:29)
And the children of Kesed also went to dwell where they could find a place, and they went and they found a valley opposite to the land of Shinar, and they dwelt there.

(Jasher 22:30)
And they there built themselves a city, and they called the name at the city Kesed after the name of their father, that is the land Kasdim to this day, and the Kasdim dwelt in that land and they were fruitful and multiplied exceedingly.

(Jasher 22:31)
And Terah, father of Nahor and Abraham, went and took another wife in his old age, and her name was Pelilah, and she conceived and bare him a son and he called his name Zoba.

(Jasher 22:32)
And Terah lived twenty-five years after he begot Zoba.

(Jasher 22:33)
And Terah died in that year, that is in the thirty-fifth year of the birth of Isaac son of Abraham.

(Jasher 22:34)
And the days of Terah were two hundred and five years, and he was buried in Haran.

(Jasher 22:35)
And Zoba the son of Terah lived thirty years and he begot

Aram, Achlis and Merik.

(Jasher 22:36)
And Aram son of Zoba son of Terah, had three wives and he begot twelve sons and three daughters; and the Lord gave to Aram the son of Zoba, riches and possessions, and abundance of cattle, and flocks and herds, and the man increased greatly.

(Jasher 22:37)
And Aram the son of Zoba and his brother and all his household journeyed from Haran, and they went to dwell where they should find a place, for their property was too great to remain in Haran; for they could not stop in Haran together with their brethren the children of Nahor.

(Jasher 22:38)
And Aram the son of Zoba went with his brethren, and they found a valley at a distance toward the eastern country and they dwelt there.

(Jasher 22:39)
And they also built a city there, and they called the name thereof Aram, after the name of their eldest brother; that is Aram Zoba to this day.

Genesis: Chapter Twenty-Three

(Jubilees 19:1)
And in the first year of the first week in the forty second jubilee, Abraham returned and dwelt opposite Hebron, that is Kirjath Arba, two weeks of years.

(Genesis 23:1) (Jasher 23:1...) (Jubilees 19:2...)
And in the first year of the third week of this jubilee the days of the life of Sarah were accomplished. And Sarah was a hundred and twenty-seven years old: these were the years of the life of Sarah.

(Genesis 23:2) (...Jasher 23:1...) (...Jubilees 19:2,3...)
And Sarah died in Kirjatharba; the same is Hebron in the land of Canaan: and Abraham came to mourn for Sarah, and to weep for her and bury her,

(...Jubilees 19:3)
And the angels tried him to see if his spirit were patient and he were not indignant in the words of his mouth; and he was found patient in this, and was not disturbed.

(Genesis 23:3) (...Jasher 23:1) (Jubilees 19:4)
And Abraham stood up from before his dead, to seek a burial place to bury his wife Sarah; and he went and in patience of spirit he spoke to the sons of Heth, the inhabitants of the land, to the intent that they should give him a place in which to bury his dead, saying,

(Genesis 23:4) (Jasher 23:2)
I am a stranger and a sojourner with you in your land; give me a possession of a burying place with you in your land, that I may bury my dead out of my sight.

(Genesis 23:5) (Jasher 23:3...)
And the children of Heth answered Abraham, saying to him,

(Genesis 23:6) (...Jasher 23:3)
Hear us, my lord: you are a mighty prince among us: behold the land is before you, in the choice of our sepulchers bury your dead; none of us shall withhold from you his sepulcher, but that you may bury your dead.

(Genesis 23:7)
And Abraham stood up, and bowed himself to the people of the land, even to the children of Heth.

(Genesis 23:8) (Jasher 23:4...)
And he communed with them, saying, If it be your mind that I should bury my dead out of my sight, if you are agreeable to this hear me, go and entreat for me to Ephron the son of Zohar,

(Genesis 23:9) (...Jasher 23:4)
Requesting that he may give me the cave of Machpelah, which he has, which is in the end of his field; and I will purchase it of him for whatever he desire for it, for as much money as it is worth he shall give it me for a possession of a burying place among you.

(Genesis 23:10) (Jasher 23:5...)
And Ephron dwelt among the children of Heth: and they went and called for him, and he came before Abraham, and Ephron

the Hittite answered Abraham in the audience of the children of Heth, even of all that went in at the gate of his city, saying,

(Genesis 23:11) (...Jasher 23:5...)
Nay, my lord, hear me: Behold all you require your servant will do; the field give I you, and the cave that is therein, I give it you; in the presence of the sons of my people give I it you: bury your dead.

(Genesis 23:12)
And Abraham bowed down himself before the people of the land.

(Genesis 23:13) (...Jasher 23:5)
And Abraham spoke to Ephron in the audience of the people of the land, saying, No, but if you will give it, I pray, hear me: I will give you money for the field which you have for value, in order that it may be for a possession of a burial place forever; take it of me, and I will bury my dead there.

(Genesis 23:14) (Jasher 23:6...)
And Ephron answered Abraham, saying to him,

(...Jasher 23:6)
Behold the field and the cave are before you, give whatever you desire; and Abraham said, Only at full value will I buy it from your hand, and from the hands of those that go in at the gate of your city, and from the hand of your seed forever.

(Genesis 23:15)
My lord, hearken to me: the land is worth four hundred shekels of silver; what is that between me and you? Bury therefore your dead.

(Genesis 23:16) (Jasher 23:7)

And Ephron and all his brethren heard this, and Abraham hearkened to Ephron; and Abraham weighed to Ephron the silver in the hands of Ephron and in the hands of all his brethren; which he had named in the audience of the sons of Heth, four hundred shekels of silver, current money with the merchant. And Abraham wrote this transaction, and he wrote it and testified it with four witnesses.

(Jasher 23:8)

And these are the names of the witnesses, Amigal son of Abishna the Hittite, Adichorom son of Ashunach the Hivite, Abdon son of Achiram the Gomerite, Bakdil the son of Abudish the Zidonite.

(Jasher 23:9)

And Abraham took the book of the purchase, and placed it in his treasures, and these are the words that Abraham wrote in the book, namely:

(Jasher 23:10)

That the cave and the field Abraham bought from Ephron the Hittite, and from his seed, and from those that go out of his city, and from their seed forever, are to be a purchase to Abraham and to his seed and to those that go forth from his loins, for a possession of a burial place forever; and he put a signet to it and testified it with witnesses.

(Genesis 23:17) (Jasher 23:11...)

And the field of Ephron, which was in Machpelah, which was before Mamre, the field, and the cave which was therein, and all the trees that were in the field, that were in all the borders round about, all that place, were made sure.

(Genesis 23:18) (...Jasher 23:11...)

To Abraham and to his seed after him, for a possession in the presence of the children of Heth, before all that went in at the gate of his city.

(Genesis 23:19) (...Jasher 23:11, 12...)

And after this, Abraham buried Sarah his wife there, in the cave of the field of Machpelah before Mamre: the same is in Hebron in the land of Canaan.

(Genesis 23:20) (...Jasher 23:12)

And that place and all its boundary, the field, and the cave that is therein, were made sure to Abraham for a possession of a burying place by the sons of Heth.

(Jubilees 19:5)

And the Lord gave him grace before all who saw him, and he besought in gentleness the sons of Heth, and they gave him the land of the double cave over against Mamre, that is Hebron, for four hundred pieces of silver.

(Jubilees 19:6)

And they besought him saying, We shall give it to you for nothing; but he would not take it from their hands for nothing, for he gave the price of the place, the money in full, and he bowed down before them twice, and after this he buried his dead in the double cave.

(Jasher 23:13)

And Abraham buried Sarah with pomp as observed at the interment of kings, and she was buried in very fine and beautiful garments.

(Jasher 23:14)
And at her bier was Shem, his sons Eber and Abimelech, together with Anar, Ashcol and Mamre, and all the grandees of the land followed her bier.

(Jasher 23:15) (Jubilees 19:7)
And the days of the life of Sarah were one hundred and twenty-seven years that is, two jubilees and four weeks and one year: these are the days of the years of the life of Sarah, and she died. And Abraham made a great and heavy mourning, and he performed the rites of mourning for seven days.

(Jasher 23:16)
And all the inhabitants of the land comforted Abraham and Isaac his son on account of Sarah.

(Jasher 23:17)
And when the days of their mourning passed by Abraham sent away his son Isaac, and he went to the house of Shem and Eber, to learn the ways of the Lord and his instructions, and Abraham remained there three years.

(Jasher 23:18)
At that time Abraham rose up with all his servants, and they went and returned homeward to Beersheba, and Abraham and all his servants remained in Beersheba.

(Jubilees 19:8)
This is the tenth trial wherewith Abraham was tried, and he was found faithful, patient in spirit.

(Jubilees 19:9)
And he said not a single word regarding the rumor in the land how that God had said that He would give it to him and to his

seed after him, and he begged a place there to bury his dead; for he was found faithful, and was recorded on the heavenly tablets as the friend of God.

(Jasher 23:19)
And at the revolution of the year Abimelech king of the Philistines died in that year; he was one hundred and ninety-three years old at his death; and Abraham went with his people to the land of the Philistines, and they comforted the whole household and all his servants, and he then turned and went home.

(Jasher 23:20)
And it was after the death of Abimelech that the people of Gerar took Benmalich his son, and he was only twelve years old, and they made him to rule in the place of his father.

(Jasher 23:21)
And they called his name Abimelech after the name of his father, for thus was it their custom to do in Gerar, and Abimelech reigned instead of Abimelech his father, and he sat upon his throne.

(Jasher 23:22)
And Lot the son of Haran also died in those days, in the thirty-ninth year of the life of Isaac, and all the days that Lot lived were one hundred and forty years and he died.

(Jasher 23:23)
And these are the children of Lot, that were born to him by his daughters, the name of the first born was Moab, and the name of the second was Benami.

(Jasher 23:24)
And the two sons of Lot went and took themselves wives from the land of Canaan, and they bore children to them, and the children of Moab were Ed, Mayon, Tarsus, and Kanvil, four sons, these are fathers to the children of Moab to this day.

(Jasher 23:25)
And all the families of the children of Lot went to dwell wherever they should light upon, for they were fruitful and increased abundantly.

(Jasher 23:26)
And they went and built themselves cities in the land where they dwelt, and they called the names of the cities which they built after their own names.

(Jasher 23:27)
And Nahor the son of Terah, brother to Abraham, died in those days in the fortieth year of the life of Isaac, and all the days of Nahor were one hundred and seventy-two years and he died and was buried in Haran.

(Jasher 23:28)
And when Abraham heard that his brother was dead he grieved sadly, and he mourned over his brother many days.

Genesis: Chapter Twenty-Four

(Genesis 24:1)
And Abraham was old, and well stricken in age: and the LORD had blessed Abraham in all things.

(Jasher 23:29)
And Abraham called for Eliezer his head servant, to give him orders concerning his house, and he came and stood before him.

(Genesis 24:2) (Jasher 23:30...)
And Abraham said to his eldest servant of his house, that ruled over all that he had, Behold I am old, I do not know the day of my death; for I am advanced in days; Put, I pray, your hand under my thigh:

(Genesis 24:3) (...Jasher 23:30)
And I will make you swear by the LORD, the God of heaven, and the God of the earth, that you shall rise up, go forth and not take a wife to my son from this place and from this land, of the daughters of the Canaanites, among whom I dwell:

(Genesis 24:4) (Jasher 23:31...)
But you shall go to my country, and to my kindred, and take a wife to my son Isaac.

(Genesis 24:5) (Jasher 23:32)
And the servant answered his master Abraham and said to him, Behold I go to your birthplace and to your father's house, and take a wife for your son from there; Peradventure the

woman will not be willing to follow me to this land: do I need to bring your son again to the land from where you came?

(Genesis 24:6) (Jasher 23:33)

And Abraham said to him, Beware, that you do not bring my son there again, for the Lord before whom I have walked he will send his angel before you and prosper your way.

(Genesis 24:7) (...Jasher 23:31)

The LORD God of heaven, which took me from my father's house, and from the land of my kindred, and brought me to this place, and which spoke to me, and that swore to me, saying, To your seed will I give this land for an inheritance forever; He shall send His angel before you, and prosper your way, and you shall take a wife to my son from there, from my family and from my father's house.

(Genesis 24:8)

And if the woman will not be willing to follow you, then you shall be clear from my oath: only do not bring my son there again.

(Genesis 24:9)

And the servant put his hand under the thigh of Abraham his master, and swore to him concerning that matter.

(Genesis 24:10) (Jasher 23:34...)

And Eliezer did as Abraham ordered him, and Eliezer swore to Abraham his master upon this matter; and Eliezer rose up. And the servant took ten camels of the camels of his master, and ten men from his master's servants with him, and departed; for all the goods of his master were in his hand: and he arose, and went to Mesopotamia, to Haran, the city of Abraham and of Nahor in order to fetch a wife for Isaac the son of Abraham.

(...Jasher 23:34)
And while they were gone Abraham sent to the house of Shem and Eber, and they brought from there his son Isaac.

(Jasher 23:35...)
And Isaac came home to his father's house to Beersheba, while Eliezer and his men came to Haran;

(Genesis 24:11) (...Jasher 23:35)
And they stopped in the city by the watering place, and he made his camels to kneel down without the city by a well of water at the time of the evening, even the time that women go out to draw water, and they remained there.

(Genesis 24:12) (Jasher 23:36)
And Eliezer, Abraham's servant, prayed, and he said, O LORD God of my master Abraham, I pray, send me good speed this day, and show kindness to my master Abraham, that you shall appoint this day a wife for my master's son from his family.

(Genesis 24:13)
Behold, I stand here by the well of water; and the daughters of the men of the city come out to draw water:

(Genesis 24:14)
And let it come to pass, that the damsel to whom I shall say, Let down your pitcher, I pray, that I may drink; and she shall say, Drink, and I will give your camels drink also: let her be the same that You have appointed for Your servant Isaac; and thereby shall I know that You have showed kindness to my master.

(Jasher 23:37...)
And the Lord hearkened to the voice of Eliezer, for the sake of his servant Abraham,

(Genesis 24:15) (...Jasher 23:36...)
And it came to pass, before he was done speaking, that, behold, Rebekah came out, who was born to Bethuel, son of Milcah, the wife of Nahor, Abraham's brother, with her pitcher on her shoulder.

(Genesis 24:16)
And the damsel was very fair to look on, a virgin, neither had any man known her: and she went down to the well, and filled her pitcher, and came up.

(Genesis 24:17)
And the servant ran to meet her, and said, Let me, I pray, drink a little water of your pitcher.

(Genesis 24:18)
And she said, Drink, my lord: and she hurried, and let down her pitcher on her hand, and gave him drink.

(Genesis 24:19)
And when she was done giving him drink, she said, I will draw water for your camels also, until they have done drinking.

(Genesis 24:20)
And she hurried, and emptied her pitcher into the trough, and ran again to the well to draw water, and drew for all his camels.

(Genesis 24:21)
And the man wondering at her held his peace, to know whether

the LORD had made his journey prosperous or not.

(Genesis 24:22)
And it came to pass, as the camels was done drinking, that the man took a golden earring of half a shekel weight, and two bracelets for her hands of ten shekels weight of gold;

(Genesis 24:23)
And said, Whose daughter are you? Tell me, I pray: is there room in your father's house for us to lodge in?

(Genesis 24:24)
And she said to him, I am the daughter of Bethuel the son of Milcah, which she bore to Nahor.

(Genesis 24:25)
She said moreover to him, We have both straw and provender enough, and room to lodge in.

(Genesis 24:26)
And the man bowed down his head, and worshipped the LORD.

(Genesis 24:27)
And he said, Blessed be the LORD God of my master Abraham, who has not left destitute my master of his mercy and his truth: I being in the way, the LORD led me to the house of my master's brethren.

(Genesis 24:28)
And the damsel ran, and told them of her mother's house these things.

(Genesis 24:29)

And Rebekah had a brother, and his name was Laban: and Laban ran out to the man, to the well.

(Genesis 24:30)

And it came to pass, when he saw the earring and bracelets on his sister's hands, and when he heard the words of Rebekah his sister, saying, Thus, the man spoke to me; that he came to the man; and, behold, he stood by the camels at the well.

(Genesis 24:31)

And he said, Come in, you blessed of the LORD; why do you stand without? For I have prepared the house, and room for the camels.

(Genesis 24:32) (...Jasher 23:37)

And the man came into the house: and he ungirded his camels, and gave straw and provender for the camels, and water to wash his feet, and the men's feet that were with him.

(Genesis 24:33)

And there was set meat before him to eat: but he said, I will not eat, until I have told my errand. And he said, Speak on.

(Jasher 23:38)

And Eliezer related to them all his concerns, and that he was Abraham's servant, and they greatly rejoiced at him.

(Genesis 24:34)

And he said, I am Abraham's servant.

(Genesis 24:35)

And the LORD has blessed my master greatly; and he is become great: and He has given him flocks, and herds, and silver, and gold, and men servants, and maidservants, and camels, and donkeys.

(Genesis 24:36)

And Sarah my master's wife bore a son to my master when she was old: and to him has he given all that he has.

(Genesis 24:37)

And my master made me swear, saying, You shall not take a wife to my son of the daughters of the Canaanites, in whose land I dwell:

(Genesis 24:38)

But you shall go to my father's house, and to my kindred, and take a wife to my son.

(Genesis 24:39)

And I said to my master, Peradventure the woman will not follow me.

(Genesis 24:40)

And he said to me, The LORD, before whom I walk, will send His angel with you, and prosper your way; and you shall take a wife for my son of my kindred, and of my father's house:

(Genesis 24:41)

Then shall you be clear from my oath, when you come to my kindred; and if they give not you one, you shall be clear from my oath.

(Genesis 24:42)

And I came this day to the well, and said, O LORD God of my master Abraham, if now You do prosper my way which I go:

(Genesis 24:43)

Behold, I stand by the well of water; and it shall come to pass, that when the virgin comes forth to draw water, and I say to her, Give me, I pray, a little water of your pitcher to drink;

(Genesis 24:44)

And she say to me, Both drink you, and I will also draw for your camels: let the same be the woman whom the LORD has appointed out for my master's son.

(Genesis 24:45)

And before I was done speaking in my heart, behold, Rebekah came forth with her pitcher on her shoulder; and she went down to the well, and drew water: and I said to her, Let me drink, I pray.

(Genesis 24:46)

And she made haste, and let down her pitcher from her shoulder, and said, Drink, and I will give your camels drink also: so I drank, and she made the camels drink also.

(Genesis 24:47)

And I asked her, and said, Whose daughter are you? And she said, The daughter of Bethuel, Nahor's son, whom Milcah bore to him: and I put the earring on her face, and the bracelets on her hands.

(Genesis 24:48)

And I bowed down my head, and worshipped the LORD, and blessed the LORD God of my master Abraham, which had led me in the right way to take my master's brother's daughter to his son.

(Genesis 24:49)

And now if you will deal kindly and truly with my master, tell me: and if not, tell me; that I may turn to the right hand, or to the left.

(Genesis 24:50)

Then Laban and Bethuel answered and said, The thing proceeds from the LORD: we cannot speak to you bad or good.

(Genesis 24:51)

Behold, Rebekah is before you, take her, and go, and let her be your master's son's wife, as the LORD has spoken.

(Genesis 24:52)

And it came to pass, that, when Abraham's servant heard their words, he worshipped the LORD, bowing himself to the earth.

(Jasher 24:39)

And they all blessed the Lord who brought this thing about, and they gave him Rebecca, the daughter of Bethuel, for a wife for Isaac.

(Jasher 24:40)

And the young woman was of very comely appearance, she was a virgin, and Rebecca was ten years old in those days.

(Genesis 24:53)

And the servant brought forth jewels of silver, and jewels of gold, and raiment, and gave them to Rebekah: he gave also to her brother and to her mother precious things.

(Genesis 24:54...) (Jasher 24:41)

And Bethuel and Laban and his children made a feast on that night, and they ate and drank, he and the men that were with him, and tarried and rejoiced there all night;

(...Genesis 24:54) (Jasher 24:42...)

And they rose up in the morning, Eliezer and the men that were with him, and he called to the whole household of Bethuel, and said, Send me away to my master.

(Genesis 24:55)

And her brother and her mother said, Let the damsel abide with us a few days, at the least ten; after that she shall go.

(Genesis 24:56)

And he said to them, Do not hinder me, seeing the LORD has prospered my way; send me away that I may go to my master.

(Genesis 24:57)

And they said, We will call the damsel, and enquire at her mouth.

(Genesis 24:58)

And they called Rebekah, and said to her, Will you go with this man? And she said, I will go.

(Genesis 24:59) (...Jasher 24:42...43...)

And they rose up and sent away Rebekah their sister, and her nurse, Deborah, the daughter of Uz, and they gave her silver and gold, men servants and maid servants, and they sent Eliezer, Abraham's servant, away and his men.

(Genesis 24:60) (...Jasher 24:42)

And they blessed Rebekah, and said to her, You are our sister, be you the mother of thousands of millions, and let your seed possess the gate of those which hate them.

(Genesis 24:61) (...Jasher 24:43)

And Rebekah arose, and her damsels, and they rode on the camels, and followed the man: and the servant took Rebekah, and went his way, and returned to his master to the land of Canaan.

(Genesis 24:62)

And Isaac came from the way of the well Lahairoi; for he dwelt in the south country.

(Genesis 24:63)

And Isaac went out to meditate in the field at the eventide: and he lifted up his eyes, and saw, and, behold, the camels were coming.

(Genesis 24:64)

And Rebekah lifted up her eyes, and when she saw Isaac, she lighted off the camel.

(Genesis 24:65)

For she had said to the servant, Who is this man that walks in the field to meet us? And the servant had said, It is my master: therefore, she took a veil, and covered herself.

(Genesis 24:66)

And the servant told Isaac all things that he was done.

(Genesis 24:67) (Jasher 24:44)

And Isaac brought her into his mother Sarah's tent, and took Rebekah, and she became his wife; and he loved her: and Isaac was comforted after his mother's death.

(Jubilees 19:10)

And in the fourth year thereof Abraham took a wife for his son

Isaac and her name was Rebecca, the daughter of Bethuel, the son of Nahor, the brother of Abraham the sister of Laban and daughter of Bethuel; and Bethuel was the son of Melca, who was the wife of Nahor, the brother of Abraham.

Genesis: Chapter Twenty-Five

(Genesis 25:1) (Jasher 25:1) (Jubilees 19:11...)

Then, it was at that time that Abraham took to himself a third wife, in his old age, and her name was Keturah, from among the daughters of his household servants, from the land of Canaan: for Hagar had died before Sarah.

(Genesis 25:2) (Jasher 25:2) (...Jubilees 19:11)

And she bore him Zimran, and Jokshan, and Medan, and Midian, and Ishbak, and Shuah, being six sons, in the two weeks of years. And the children of Zimran were Abihen, Molich and Narim.

(Genesis 25:3) (Jasher 25:3...)

And Jokshan begot Sheba, and Dedan. And the sons of Dedan were Asshurim, and Letushim, and Leummim.

(...Jasher 25:3...)

And the sons of Medan were Amida, Joab, Gochi, Elisha and Nothach;

(Genesis 25:4...) (...Jasher 25:3)

And the sons of Midian; Ephah, and Epher, and Hanoch, and Abida, and Eldaah.

(Jasher 25:4)

And the sons of Ishbak were Makiro, Beyodua and Tator.

(...Genesis 25:4) (Jasher 25:5)

And the sons of Shuach were Bildad, Mamdad, Munan and

Meban; All these were the families of the children of Keturah the Canaanitish woman which she bare to Abraham the Hebrew.

(Genesis 25:5)

And Abraham gave all that he had to Isaac.

(Genesis 25:6) (Jasher 25:6, 7)

But to the sons of the concubines, which Abraham had, Abraham gave gifts, and sent them away and they went away from Isaac his son, while he yet lived, to dwell wherever they should find a place, And all these went to the mountain eastward, to the east country. And they built themselves six cities in which they dwelt to this day.

(Jasher 25:8)
But the children of Sheba and Dedan, children of Jokshan, with their children, did not dwell with their brethren in their cities, and they journeyed and encamped in the countries and wildernesses to this day.

(Jasher 25:9)
And the children of Midian, son of Abraham, went to the east of the land of Cush, and they there found a large valley in the eastern country, and they remained there and built a city, and they dwelt therein, that is the land of Midian to this day.

(Jasher 25:10)
And Midian dwelt in the city which he built, he and his five sons and all belonging to him.

(Jasher 25:11)
And these are the names of the sons of Midian according to their names in their cities, Ephah, Epher, Chanoch, Abida

and Eldaah.

(Jasher 25:12)
And the sons of Ephah were Methach, Meshar, Avi and Tzanua, and the sons of Epher were Ephron, Zur, Alirun and Medin, and the sons of Chanoch were Reuel, Rekem, Azi, Alyoshub and Alad.

(Jasher 25:13)
And the sons of Abida were Chur, Melud, Kerury, Molchi; and the sons of Eldaah were Miker, and Reba, and Malchiyah and Gabol; these are the names of the Midianites according to their families; and afterward the families of Midian spread throughout the land of Midian.

(Genesis 25:7) (Jasher 26:29...)
And these are all the days of the years of Abraham's life which he lived, a hundred, and seventy-five years.

(Genesis 25:8) (...Jasher 26:29...)
Then it was at that time that Abraham gave up the ghost, and died in the fifteenth year of the life of Jacob and Esau, the sons of Isaac, in a good old age, an old man and satisfied with days, and full of years; and was gathered to his people.

(Genesis 25:9) (...Jasher 26:29)
And his sons Isaac and Ishmael buried him in the cave of Machpelah, in the field of Ephron the son of Zohar the Hittite, which is before Mamre;

(Jasher 26:30)
And when the inhabitants of Canaan heard that Abraham was dead, they all came with their kings and princes and all their men to bury Abraham.

(Genesis 25:10) (Jasher 26:31)
And all the inhabitants of the land of Haran, and all the families of the house of Abraham, and all the princes and grandees, and the sons of Abraham by the concubines, all came when they heard of Abraham's death, and they requited Abraham's kindness, and comforted Isaac his son, and they buried Abraham in the cave the field which Abraham purchased from Ephron the Hittite and his children, of the sons of Heth which he bought for the possession of a burial place: there was Abraham buried, and Sarah his wife.

(Jasher 26:32)
And all the inhabitants of Canaan, and all those who had known Abraham, wept for Abraham a whole year, and men and women mourned over him.

(Jasher 26:33)
And all the little children, and all the inhabitants of the land wept on account of Abraham, for Abraham had been good to them all, and because he had been upright with God and men.

(Jasher 26:34)
And there arose not a man who feared God like to Abraham, for he had feared his God from his youth, and had served the Lord, and had gone in all his ways during his life, from his childhood to the day of his death.

(Jasher 26:35)
And the Lord was with him and delivered him from the counsel of Nimrod and his people, and when he made war with the four kings of Elam he conquered them.

(Jasher 26:36)
And he brought all the children of the earth to the service of

God, and he taught them the ways of the Lord, and caused them to know the Lord.

(Jasher 26:37)
And he formed a grove and he planted a vineyard therein, and he had always prepared in his tent meat and drink to those that passed through the land, that they might satisfy themselves in his house.

(Jasher 26:38)
And the Lord God delivered the whole earth on account of Abraham. And it was after the death of Abraham that God blessed his son Isaac

(Genesis 25:11) (Jasher 26:39)
And it came to pass after the death of Abraham, that God blessed his son Isaac; and his children, and the Lord was with Isaac as he had been with his father Abraham, for Isaac kept all the commandments of the Lord as Abraham his father had commanded him; he did not turn to the right or to the left from the right path which his father had commanded him. And Isaac dwelt by the well Lahairoi.

(Genesis 25:12) (Jasher 25:14)
Now these are the generations of Ishmael, Abraham's son, whom Hagar the Egyptian, Sarah's handmaid, bore to Abraham:

(Jasher 25:15)
And Ishmael took a wife from the land of Egypt, and her name was Ribah, the same is Meribah.

(Genesis 25:13) (Jasher 25:16)
And these are the names of the sons of Ishmael, by their

names, according to their generations: and Ribah bore to Ishmael the firstborn of Ishmael, Nebajoth; and Kedar, and Adbeel, and Mibsam, and their sister Bosmath.

(Jasher 25:17)
And Ishmael cast away his wife Ribah, and she went from him and returned to Egypt to the house of her father, and she dwelt there, for she had been very bad in the sight of Ishmael, and in the sight of his father Abraham.

(Genesis 25:14) (Jasher 25:18...)
And Ishmael afterward took a wife from the land of Canaan, and her name was Malchuth, and she bare to him Mishma, and Dumah, and Massa,

(Genesis 25:15) (...Jasher 25:18)
Hadar, and Tema, Jetur, Naphish, and Kedemah:

(Genesis 25:16) (Jasher 25:19)
These are the sons of Ishmael, and these are their names, by their towns, and by their castles; twelve princes according to their nations; and the families of Ishmael afterward spread forth, and Ishmael took his children and all the property that he had gained, together with the souls of his household and all belonging to him, and they went to dwell where they should find a place.

(Genesis 25:17)
And these are the years of the life of Ishmael, a hundred and thirty and seven years: and he gave up the ghost and died; and was gathered to his people.

(Genesis 25:18) (Jasher 25:20)
And they went and dwelt near the wilderness of Paran, they

dwelt from Havilah to Shur, that is before Egypt, as you go toward Assyria: and Abraham died in the presence of all his brethren.

(Jasher 25:21)
And Ishmael and his sons dwelt in the land, and they had children born to them, and they were fruitful and increased abundantly.

(Jasher 25:22)
And these are the names of the sons of Nebayoth the first born of Ishmael; Mend, Send, Mayon; and the sons of Kedar were Alyon, Kezem, Chamad and Eli.

(Jasher 25:23)
And the sons of Adbeel were Chamad and Jabin; and the sons of Mibsam were Obadiah, Ebedmelech and Yeush; these are the families of the children of Ribah the wife of Ishmael.

(Jasher 25:24)
And the sons of Mishma the son of Ishmael were Shamua, Zecaryon and Obed; and the sons of Dumah were Kezed, Eli, Machmad and Amed.

(Jasher 25:25)
And the sons of Masa were Melon, Mula and Ebidadon; and the sons of Chadad were Azur, Minzar and Ebedmelech; and the sons of Tema were Seir, Sadon and Yakol.

(Jasher 25:26)
And the sons of Yetur were Merith, Yaish, Alyo, and Pachoth; and the sons of Naphish were Ebed-Tamed, Abiyasaph and Mir; and the sons of Kedma were Calip, Tachti, and Omir;

these were the children of Malchuth the wife of Ishmael according to their families.

(Jasher 25:27)
All these are the families of Ishmael according to their generations, and they dwelt in those lands wherein they had built themselves cities to this day.

(Genesis 25:19)

And these are the generations of Isaac, Abraham's son: Abraham begot Isaac:

(Genesis 25:20) (Jasher 24:45)

And Isaac was forty years old when he took Rebekah to wife, the daughter of his uncle Bethuel the Syrian of Padanaram, the sister to Laban the Syrian.

(Jasher 25:28)
And Rebecca the daughter of Bethuel, the wife of Abraham's son Isaac, was barren in those days, she had no offspring; and Isaac dwelt with his father in the land of Canaan; and the Lord was with Isaac; and Arpachshad the son of Shem the son of Noah died in those days, in the forty-eighth year of the life of Isaac, and all the days that Arpachshad lived were four hundred and thirty-eight years, and he died.

(Jasher 26:1)
And in the fifty-ninth year of the life of Isaac the son of Abraham, Rebecca his wife was still barren in those days.

(Jasher 26:2)
And Rebecca said to Isaac, Truly I have heard, my lord, that your mother Sarah was barren in her days until my Lord

Abraham, your father, prayed for her and she conceived by him.

(Jasher 26:3)
Now therefore stand up, pray you also to God and he will hear your prayer and remember us through his mercies.

(Jasher 26:4)
And Isaac answered his wife Rebecca, saying, Abraham has already prayed for me to God to multiply his seed, now therefore this barrenness must proceed to us from you.

(Jasher 26:5...)
And Rebecca said to him, But arise now you also and pray, that the Lord may hear your prayer and grant me children, and Isaac hearkened to the words of his wife, and Isaac and his wife rose up and went to the land of Moriah to pray there and to seek the Lord,

(Genesis 25:21...) (...Jasher 26:5)
And when they had reached that place Isaac stood up and Isaac entreated the LORD for his wife, because she was barren:

(Jasher 26:6)
And Isaac said, O Lord God of heaven and earth, Whose goodness and mercies fill the earth, You who took my father from his father's house and from his birthplace, and brought him to this land, and said to him, To your seed will I give the land, and You promised him and declared to him, I will multiply your seed as the stars of heaven and as the sand of the sea, now may Your words be verified which You spoke to my father.

(Jasher 26:7)
For You are the Lord our God, our eyes are toward You to give us seed of men, as You promised us, for You are the Lord our God and our eyes are directed toward You only.

(...Genesis 25:21) (Jasher 26:8)
And the Lord heard the prayer of Isaac the son of Abraham, and the LORD was entreated of him, and Rebekah his wife conceived.

(Genesis 25:22) (Jasher 26:9)
And in about seven months after the children struggled together within her; and it pained her greatly that she was wearied on account of them, and she said to all the women who were then in the land, Did such a thing happen to you as it has to me? And they said to her, No.

(Genesis 25:22) (Jasher 26:10)
And she said to them, If it be so, why am I thus? Why am I alone in this among all the women that were upon earth? And she went to the land of Moriah to enquire of the LORD on account of this; and she went to Shem and Eber his son to make inquiries of them in this matter, and that they should seek the Lord in this thing respecting her.

(Jasher 26:11)
And she also asked Abraham to seek and inquire of the Lord about all that had befallen her.

(Genesis 25:23) (Jasher 26:12)
And they all inquired of the Lord concerning this matter, and they brought her word from the LORD and said to her, Two children are in your womb, and two nations shall rise from them; and two manner of people shall be separated from your

bowels; and the one people shall be stronger than the other people; and the elder shall serve the younger.

(Genesis 25:24) (Jasher 26:13)
And when her days to be delivered were fulfilled, she knelt down, and behold, there were twins in her womb, as the Lord had spoken to her.

(Genesis 25:25) (Jasher 26:14)
And the first came out red, all over like a hairy garment; and they and all the people of the land called his name Esau, saying, That this one was made complete from the womb.

(Genesis 25:26) (Jasher 26:15, 16)
And after that his brother came out, and his hand took hold on Esau's heel; and his name was called Jacob: and Isaac, the son of Abraham, was sixty years old when she bore them.

(Jubilees 19:12)
And in the sixth week, in the second year thereof, Rebecca bare to Isaac two sons, Jacob and Esau.

~ ~ ~

(Jasher 26:18)
And Isaac and the children of his household dwelt with his father Abraham in the land of Canaan, as God had commanded them.

(Jasher 26:19)
And Ishmael the son of Abraham went with his children and

all belonging to them, and they returned there to the land of Havilah, and they dwelt there.

(Jasher 26:20)
And all the children of Abraham's concubines went to dwell in the land of the east, for Abraham had sent them away from his son, and had given them presents, and they went away.

(Jasher 26:21)
And Abraham gave all that he had to his son Isaac, and he also gave him all his treasures.

(Jasher 26:22)
And he commanded him saying, Do you not know and understand the Lord is God in heaven and in earth, and there is no other beside him?

(Jasher 26:23)
And it was he who took me from my father's house, and from my birth place, and gave me all the delights upon earth; who delivered me from the counsel of the wicked, for in him I trusted.

(Jasher 26:24)
And he brought me to this place, and he delivered me from Ur Casdim; and he said to me, To your seed will I give all these lands, and they shall inherit them when they keep my commandments, my statutes and my judgments that I have commanded you, and which I shall command them.

(Jasher 26:25)
Now therefore my son, hearken to my voice, and keep the commandments of the Lord your God, which I commanded you, do not turn from the right way either to the right or to the

left, in order that it may be well with you and your children after you forever.

(Jasher 26:26)
And remember the wonderful works of the Lord, and his kindness that he has shown toward us, in having delivered us from the hands of our enemies, and the Lord our God caused them to fall into our hands; and now therefore keep all that I have commanded you, and turn not away from the commandments of your God, and serve none beside him, in order that it may be well with you and your seed after you.

(Jasher 26:27)
And teach you your children and your seed the instructions of the Lord and his commandments, and teach them the upright way in which they should go, in order that it may be well with them forever.

(Jasher 26:28...)
And Isaac answered his father and said to him, That which my Lord has commanded that will I do, and I will not depart from the commands of the Lord my God, I will keep all that he commanded me;

~ ~ ~

(Genesis 25:27) (Jasher 26:17) (Jubilees 19:13, 14...)
And the boys grew up to their fifteenth year, and they came among the society of men: and Esau was fierce, a designing and deceitful man, and an expert, cunning hunter, a man of the field, and hairy; and Jacob was a plain man, a smooth and upright man, perfect and wise, dwelling in tents, feeding flocks

and learning the instructions of the Lord and the commands of his father and mother.

(...Jubilees 19:14)
And Jacob learned to write; but Esau did not learn, for he was a man of the field and a hunter, and he learned war, and all his deeds were fierce.

(Genesis 25:28) (Jubilees 19:15, 16)

And Abraham loved Jacob, but Isaac loved Esau, because he ate of his venison. And Abraham saw the deeds of Esau, and he knew that in Jacob should his name and seed be called; and he called Rebecca and gave commandment regarding Jacob, for he knew that Rebekah loved Jacob much more than Esau.

(Jubilees 19:17)
And Abraham said to her: My daughter, watch over my son Jacob, For he shall be in my stead on the earth, And for a blessing in the midst of the children of men, And for the glory of the whole seed of Shem.

(Jubilees 19:18)
For I know that the Lord will choose him to be a people for possession to Himself, above all peoples that are on the face of the earth.

(Jubilees 19:19)
And behold, Isaac my son loves Esau more than Jacob, but I see that you truly love Jacob.

(Jubilees 19:20)
Add still further to your kindness to him, and let your eyes be on him in love; for he shall be a blessing to us on the earth from here after, to all generations of the earth.

(Jubilees 19:21)
Let your hands be strong and let your heart rejoice in your son Jacob; for I have loved him far beyond all my sons. He shall be blessed forever, and his seed shall fill the whole earth.

(Jubilees 19:22)
If a man can number the sand of the earth, His seed also shall be numbered.

(Jubilees 19:23)
And all the blessings wherewith the Lord has blessed me and my seed shall belong to Jacob and his seed always.

(Jubilees 19:24)
And in his seed, shall my name be blessed, and the name of my fathers, Shem, and Noab, and Enoch, and Mahalalel, and Enos, and Seth, and Adam.

(Jubilees 19:25)
And these shall serve to lay the foundations of the heaven, and to strengthen the earth, and to renew all the luminaries which are in the firmament.

(Jubilees 19:26)
And he called Jacob before the eyes of Rebecca his mother, and kissed him, and blessed him, and said:

(Jubilees 19:27)
Jacob, my beloved son, whom my soul loves, may God bless you from above the firmament, and may He give you all the blessings wherewith He blessed Adam, and Enoch, and Noah, and Shem; and all the things of which He told me, and all the things which He promised to give me, may He cause to

cleave to you and to your seed forever, according to the days of heaven above the earth.

(Jubilees 19:28)
And the Spirits of Mastêmâ shall not rule over you or over your seed to turn you from the Lord, who is your God from here after, forever.

(Jubilees 19:29)
And may the Lord God be a father to you and you the first-born son, and to the people always.

(Jubilees 19:30)
Go in peace, my son. And they both went forth together from Abraham.

(...Jasher 26:28)
And Abraham blessed his son Isaac, and also his children; and Abraham taught Jacob the instruction of the Lord and his ways.

(Jubilees 19:31)
And Rebecca loved Jacob, with all her heart and with all her soul, very much more than Esau; but Isaac loved Esau much more than Jacob.

~ ~ ~

(Jubilees 20:1)
And in the forty-second jubilee, in the first year of the seventh week, Abraham called Ishmael, and his twelve sons, and Isaac

and his two sons, and the six sons of Keturah, and their sons.

(Jubilees 20:2)
And he commanded them that they should observe the way of the Lord; that they should work righteousness, and love each his neighbor, and act on this manner among all men; that they should each so walk with regard to them as to do judgment and righteousness on the earth.

(Jubilees 20:3)
That they should circumcise their sons, according to the covenant which He had made with them, and not deviate to the right hand or the left of all the paths which the Lord had commanded us; and that we should keep ourselves from all fornication and uncleanness, and renounce from among us all fornication and uncleanness.

(Jubilees 20:4)
And if any woman or maid commit fornication among you, burn her with fire and let them not commit fornication with her after their eyes and their heart; and let them not take to themselves wives from the daughters of Canaan; for the seed of Canaan will be rooted out of the land.

(Jubilees 20:5)
And he told them of the judgment of the giants, and the judgment of the Sodomites, how they had been judged on account of their wickedness, and had died on account of their fornication, and uncleanness, and mutual corruption through fornication.

(Jubilees 20:6)
And guard yourselves from all fornication and uncleanness, and from all pollution of sin, lest you make our name a curse,

and your whole life a hissing, And all your sons to be destroyed by the sword, and you become accursed like Sodom, and all your remnant as the sons of Gomorrah.

(Jubilees 20:7)
I implore you, my sons, love the God of heaven and cleave you to all His commandments. And walk not after their idols, and after their uncleanness,

(Jubilees 20:8)
And make not for yourselves molten or graven gods; For they are vanity, and there is no spirit in them; for they are work of men's hands, and all who trust in them, trust in nothing.

(Jubilees 20:9)
Serve them not, nor worship them, but serve you the Most High God, and worship Him continually: and hope for His countenance always, and work uprightness and righteousness before Him, that He may have pleasure in you and grant you His mercy, and send rain on you morning and evening, and bless all your works which you have wrought on the earth, and bless your bread and your water, and bless the fruit of your womb and the fruit of your land, and the herds of your cattle, and the flocks of your sheep.

(Jubilees 20:10)
And you will be for a blessing on the earth, and all nations of the earth will desire you, and bless your sons in my name, that they may be blessed as I am.

(Jubilees 20:11)
And he gave to Ishmael and to his sons, and to the sons of Keturah, gifts, and sent them away from Isaac his son, and he gave everything to Isaac his son.

(Jubilees 20:12)
And Ishmael and his sons, and the sons of Keturah and their sons, went together and dwelt from Paran to the entering in of Babylon in all the land which is towards the East facing the desert.

(Jubilees 20:13)
And these mingled with each other, and their name was called Arabs, and Ishmaelites.

~ ~ ~

(Jubilees 21:1)
And in the sixth year of the seventh week of this jubilee Abraham called Isaac his son, and commanded him: saying, I am become old, and know not the day of my death, and am full of my days.

(Jubilees 21:2)
And behold, I am one hundred and seventy-five years old, and throughout all the days of my life I have remembered the Lord, and sought with all my heart to do His will, and to walk uprightly in all His ways.

(Jubilees 21:3)
My soul has hated idols, and I have despised those that served them, and I have given my heart and spirit that I might observe to do the will of Him Who created me.

(Jubilees 21:4)
For He is the living God, and He is holy and faithful, and He is righteous beyond all, and there is with Him no accepting

of persons and no accepting of gifts; for God is righteous, and executes judgment on all those who transgress His commandments and despise His covenant.

(Jubilees 21:5)
And you, my son, observe His commandments and His ordinances and His judgments, and walk not after the abominations and after the graven images and after the molten images.

(Jubilees 21:6)
And eat no blood at all of animals or cattle, or of any bird which flies in the heaven.

(Jubilees 21:7)
And if you do slay a victim as an acceptable peace offering, slay it, and pour out its blood on the altar, and all the fat of the offering offer on the altar with fine flour and the meat offering mingled with oil, with its drink offering offer them all together on the altar of burnt offering; it is a sweet savor before the Lord.

(Jubilees 21:8)
And you will offer the fat of the sacrifice of thank offerings on the fire which is on the altar, and the fat which is on the belly, and all the fat on the inwards and the two kidneys, and all the fat that is on them, and on the loins and liver you shall remove, together with the kidneys.

(Jubilees 21:9)
And offer all these for a sweet savor acceptable before the Lord, with its meat-offering and with its drink- offering, for a sweet savor, the bread of the offering to the Lord.

(Jubilees 21:10)
And eat its meat on that day and on the second day, and let not the sun on the second day go down on it till it is eaten, and let nothing be left over for the third day; for it is not acceptable for it is not approved and let it no longer be eaten, and all who eat thereof will bring sin on themselves; for thus I have found it written in the books of my forefathers, and in the words of Enoch, and in the words of Noah.

(Jubilees 21:11)
And on all your oblations you shall strew salt, and let not the salt of the covenant be lacking in all your oblations before the Lord.

(Jubilees 21:12)
And as regards the wood of the sacrifices, beware lest you bring wood for the altar in addition to these: cypress, bay, almond, fir, pine, cedar, savin, fig, olive, myrrh, laurel, aspalathus.

(Jubilees 21:13)
And of these kinds of wood lay on the altar under the sacrifice, such as have been tested as to their appearance, and do not lay thereon any split or dark wood, but hard and clean, without fault, a sound and new growth; and do not lay thereon old wood, for its fragrance is gone for there is no longer fragrance in it as before.

(Jubilees 21:14)
Besides these kinds of wood there is none other that you shall place on the altar, for the fragrance is dispersed, and the smell of its fragrance goes not up to heaven.

(Jubilees 21:15)
Observe this commandment and do it, my son, that you may be upright in all your deeds.

(Jubilees 21:16)
And at all times be clean in your body, and wash yourself with water before you approach to offer on the altar, and wash your hands and your feet before you draw near to the altar; and when you are done sacrificing, wash again your hands and your feet.

(Jubilees 21:17)
And let no blood appear on you nor on your clothes; be on your guard, my son, against blood, be on your guard exceedingly; cover it with dust.

(Jubilees 21:18)
And do not eat any blood for it is the soul; eat no blood whatever.

(Jubilees 21:19)
And take no gifts for the blood of man, lest it be shed with impunity, without judgment; for it is the blood that is shed that causes the earth to sin, and the earth cannot be cleansed from the blood of man save by the blood of him who shed it.

(Jubilees 21:20)
And take no present or gift for the blood of man: blood for blood, that you may be accepted before the Lord, the Most High God; for He is the defense of the good: and that you may be preserved from all evil, and that He may save you from every kind of death.

(Jubilees 21:21)
I see, my son, That all the works of the children of men are sin and wickedness, and all their deeds are uncleanness and an abomination and a pollution, and there is no righteousness with them.

(Jubilees 21:22)
Beware, lest you should walk in their ways And tread in their paths, and sin a sin to death before the Most High God. Else He will hide His face from you and give you back into the hands of your transgression, And root you out of the land, and your seed likewise from under heaven, And your name and your seed shall perish from the whole earth.

(Jubilees 21:23)
Turn away from all their deeds and all their uncleanness, And observe the ordinance of the Most High God, And do His will and be upright in all things.

(Jubilees 21:24)
And He will bless you in all your deeds, and will raise up from you a plant of righteousness through all the earth, throughout all generations of the earth, and my name and your name shall not be forgotten under heaven forever.

(Jubilees 21:25)
Go, my son in peace. May the Most High God, my God and your God, strengthen you to do His will, and may He bless all your seed and the residue of your seed for the generations forever, with all righteous blessings, that you may be a blessing on all the earth. And he went out from him rejoicing.

~ ~ ~

(Jubilees 22:1)
And it came to pass in the first week in the forty-fourth jubilee, in the second year, that is, the year in which Abraham died, that Isaac and Ishmael came from the Well of the Oath to celebrate the feast of weeks -that is, the feast of the first fruits of the harvest-to Abraham, their father, and Abraham rejoiced because his two sons had come.

(Jubilees 22:2)
For Isaac had many possessions in Beersheba, and Isaac was wont to go and see his possessions and to return to his father.

(Jubilees 22:3)
And in those days Ishmael came to see his father, and they both came together, and Isaac offered a sacrifice for a burnt offering, and presented it on the altar of his father which he had made in Hebron.

(Jubilees 22:4)
And he offered a thank offering and made a feast of joy before Ishmael, his brother: and Rebecca made new cakes from the new grain, and gave them to Jacob, her son, to take them to Abraham, his father, from the first fruits of the land, that he might eat and bless the Creator of all things before he died.

(Jubilees 22:5)
And Isaac, too, sent by the hand of Jacob to Abraham a best thank offering, that he might eat and drink.

(Jubilees 22:6)
And he eat and drank, and blessed the Most High God, Who has created heaven and earth, Who has made all the fat things of the earth, and given them to the children of men that they might eat and drink and bless their Creator.

(Jubilees 22:7)
And now I give thanks to You, my God, because You have caused me to see this day: behold, I am one hundred and seventy-five years, an old man and full of days, and all my days have been to me peace.

(Jubilees 22:8)
The sword of the adversary has not overcome me in all that You have given me and my children all the days of my life until this day.

(Jubilees 22:9)
My God, may Your mercy and Your peace be on Your servant, and on the seed of his sons, that they may be to You a chosen nation and an inheritance from among all the nations of the earth from here after, to all the days of the generations of the earth, to all the ages.

(Jubilees 22:10)
And he called Jacob and said: My son Jacob, may the God of all bless you and strengthen you to do righteousness, and His will before Him, and may He choose you and your seed that you may become a people for His inheritance according to His will always.

(Jubilees 22:11)
And do you, my son, Jacob, draw near and kiss me. And he drew near and kissed him, and he said: Blessed be my son Jacob and all the sons of God Most High, to all the ages: May God give to you a seed of righteousness; and some of your sons may He sanctify in the midst of the whole earth; May nations serve you, and all the nations bow themselves before your seed.

(Jubilees 22:12)
Be strong in the presence of men, and exercise authority over all the seed of Seth. Then your ways and the ways of your sons will be justified, so that they shall become a holy nation.

(Jubilees 22:13)
May the Most High God give you all the blessings wherewith He has blessed me and wherewith He blessed Noah and Adam; May they rest on the sacred head of your seed from generation to generation forever.

(Jubilees 22:14)
And may He cleanse you from all unrighteousness and impurity, that you may be forgiven all the transgressions; which you have committed ignorantly. And may He strengthen you, and bless you. And may you inherit the whole earth,

(Jubilees 22:15)
And may He renew His covenant with you. That you may be to Him a nation for His inheritance for all the ages, and that He may be to you and to your seed a God in truth and righteousness throughout all the days of the earth.

(Jubilees 22:16)
And do you, my son Jacob, remember my words, and observe the commandments of Abraham, your father: Separate yourself from the nations, and eat not with them: and do not according to their works, and become not their associate; for their works are unclean, and all their ways are a Pollution and an abomination and uncleanness.

(Jubilees 22:17)
They offer their sacrifices to the dead and they worship evil spirits, and they eat over the graves, and all their works are

vanity and nothingness.

(Jubilees 22:18)
They have no heart to understand and their eyes do not see what their works are, and how they err in saying to a piece of wood: You are my God, and to a stone: You are my Lord and you are my deliverer. And they have no heart.

(Jubilees 22:19)
And as for you, my son Jacob, may the Most High God help you and the God of heaven bless you and remove you from their uncleanness and from all their error.

(Jubilees 22:20)
Beware, my son Jacob, of taking a wife from any seed of the daughters of Canaan; for all his seed is to be rooted out of the earth.

(Jubilees 22:21)
For, owing to the transgression of Ham, Canaan erred, And all his seed shall be destroyed from off the earth and all the residue thereof, and none springing from him shall be saved on the day of judgment.

(Jubilees 22:22)
And as for all the worshippers of idols and the profane, there shall be no hope for them in the land of the living; And there shall be no remembrance of them on the earth; for they shall descend into Sheol, and into the place of condemnation they shall go, as the children of Sodom were taken away from the earth So will all those who worship idols be taken away.

(Jubilees 22:23)
Fear not, my son Jacob, and be not dismayed, O son of

Abraham: may the Most High God preserve you from destruction, and from all the paths of error may He deliver you.

(Jubilees 22:24)
This house have I built for myself that I might put my name on it in the earth: it is given to you and to your seed forever, and it will be named the house of Abraham; it is given to you and to your seed forever; for you will build my house and establish my name before God forever: your seed and your name will stand throughout all generations of the earth.

(Jubilees 22:5)
And he ceased commanding him and blessing him.

(Jubilees 22:26)
And the two lay together on one bed, and Jacob slept in the bosom of Abraham, his father's father and he kissed him seven times, and his affection and his heart rejoiced over him.

(Jubilees 22:27)
And he blessed him with all his heart and said: 'The Most High God, the God of all, and Creator of all, Who brought me forth from Ur of the Chaldees that he might give me this land to inherit it forever, and that I might establish a holy seed blessed be the Most High forever.

(Jubilees 22:28)
And he blessed Jacob and said: My son, over whom with all my heart and my affection I rejoice, may Your grace and Your mercy be lift up on him and on his seed always.

(Jubilees 22:29)
And do not forsake him, nor set him at nought from here

after, to the days of eternity, and may Your eyes be opened on him and on his seed, that You may preserve him, and bless him, and may sanctify him as a nation for Your inheritance;

(Jubilees 22:30)
And bless him with all Your blessings from here after, to all the days of eternity, and renew Your covenant and Your grace with him and with his seed according to all Your good pleasure to all the generations of the earth.

~ ~ ~

(Jubilees 23:1)
And he placed two fingers of Jacob on his eyes, and he blessed the God of gods, and he covered his face and stretched out his feet and slept the sleep of eternity, and was gathered to his fathers.

(Jubilees 23:2)
And notwithstanding all this Jacob was lying in his bosom, and knew not that Abraham, his father's father, was dead.

(Jubilees 23:3)
And Jacob awoke from his sleep, and behold Abraham was cold as ice, and he said Father, father; but there was none that spoke, and he knew that he was dead.

(Jubilees 23:4)
And he arose from his bosom and ran and told Rebecca, his mother; and Rebecca went to Isaac in the night, and told him; and they went together, and Jacob with them, and a lamp was

in his hand, and when they had gone in they found Abraham lying dead.

(Jubilees 23:5)
And Isaac fell on the face of his father and wept and kissed him.

(Jubilees 23:6)
And the voices were heard in the house of Abraham, and Ishmael his son arose, and went to Abraham his father, and wept over Abraham his father, he and all the house of Abraham, and they wept with a great weeping.

(Jubilees 23:7)
And his sons Isaac and Ishmael buried him in the double cave, near Sarah his wife, and they wept for him forty days, all the men of his house, and Isaac and Ishmael, and all their sons, and all the sons of Keturah in their places; and the days of weeping for Abraham were ended.

(Jubilees 23:8)
And he lived three jubilees and four weeks of years, one hundred and seventy-five years, and completed the days of his life, being old and full of days.

(Jubilees 23:9)
For the days of the forefathers, of their life, were nineteen jubilees; and after the Flood they began to grow less than nineteen jubilees, and to decrease in jubilees, and to grow old quickly, and to be full of their days by reason of manifold tribulation and the wickedness of their ways, with the exception of Abraham.

(Jubilees 23:10)
For Abraham was perfect in all his deeds with the Lord, and well-pleasing in righteousness all the days of his life; and behold, he did not complete four jubilees in his life, when he had grown old by reason of the wickedness, and was full of his days.

(Jubilees 23:11)
And all the generations which shall arise from this time until the day of the great judgment shall grow old quickly, before they complete two jubilees, and their knowledge shall forsake them by reason of their old age and all their knowledge shall vanish away.

(Jubilees 23:12)
And in those days, if a man live a jubilee and a-half of years, they shall say regarding him: he has lived long, and the greater part of his days are pain and sorrow and tribulation. And there is no peace:

(Jubilees 23:13)
For calamity follows on calamity, and wound on wound, and tribulation on tribulation, and evil tidings on evil tidings, and illness on illness, and all evil judgments such as these, one with another, illness and overthrow, and snow and frost and ice, and fever, and chills, and torpor, and famine, and death, and sword, and captivity, and all kinds of calamities and pains.

(Jubilees 23:14)
And all these shall come on an evil generation, which transgresses on the earth: their works are uncleanness and fornication, and pollution and abominations.

(Jubilees 23:15)
Then they shall say: The days of the forefathers were many (even) to a thousand years, and were good; but behold, the days of our life, if a man has lived many, are seventy years, and, if he is strong, eighty years, and those evil, and there is no peace in the days of this evil generation.

(Jubilees 23:16)
And in that generation the sons shall convict their fathers and their elders of sin and unrighteousness, and of the words of their mouth and the great wickedness which they perpetrate, and concerning their forsaking the covenant which the Lord made between them and Him, that they should observe and do all His commandments and His ordinances and all His laws, without departing either to the right hand or the left.

(Jubilees 23:17)
For all have done evil, and every mouth speaks iniquity and all their works are an uncleanness and an abomination, and all their ways are pollution, uncleanness and destruction.

(Jubilees 23:18)
Behold the earth shall be destroyed on account of all their works, and there shall be no seed of the vine, and no oil; for their works are altogether faithless, and they shall all perish together, beasts and cattle and birds, and all the fish of the sea, on account of the children of men.

(Jubilees 23:19)
And they shall strive one with another, the young with the old, and the old with the young, the poor with the rich, the lowly with the great, and the beggar with the prince, on account of the law and the covenant; for they have forgotten commandment, and covenant, and feasts, and months, and Sabbaths, and jubilees, and all judgments.

(Jubilees 23:20)
And they shall stand with bows and swords and war to turn them back into the way; but they shall not return until much blood has been shed on the earth, one by another.

(Jubilees 23:21)
And those who have escaped shall not return from their wickedness to the way of righteousness, but they shall all exalt themselves to deceit and wealth, that they may each take all that is his neighbor's, and they shall name the great name, but not in truth and not in righteousness, and they shall defile the holy of holies with their uncleanness and the corruption of their pollution.

(Jubilees 23:22)
And a great punishment shall befall the deeds of this generation from the Lord, and He will give them over to the sword and to judgment and to captivity, and to be plundered and devoured.

(Jubilees 23:23)
And He will wake up against them the sinners of the Gentiles, who have neither mercy nor compassion, and who shall respect the person of none, neither old nor young, nor anyone, for they are more wicked and strong to do evil than all the children of men. And they shall use violence against Israel and transgression against Jacob, And much blood shall be shed on the earth, And there shall be none to gather and none to bury.

(Jubilees 23:24)
In those days they shall cry aloud, And call and pray that they may be saved from the hand of the sinners, the Gentiles; but none shall be saved.

(Jubilees 23:25)
And the heads of the children shall be white with gray hair, and a child of three weeks shall appear old like a man of one hundred years, and their stature shall be destroyed by tribulation and oppression.

(Jubilees 23:26)
And in those days the children shall begin to study the laws, and to seek the commandments, and to return to the path of righteousness.

(Jubilees 23:27)
And the days shall begin to grow many and increase among those children of men till their days draw nigh to one thousand years. And to a greater number of years than was the number of the days.

(Jubilees 23:28)
And there shall be no old man nor one who is not satisfied with his days, for all shall be children and youths.

(Jubilees 23:29)
And all their days they shall complete and live in peace and in joy, and there shall be no Satan nor any evil destroyer; For all their days shall be days of blessing and healing.

(Jubilees 23:30)
And at that time the Lord will heal His servants, and they shall rise up and see great peace, and drive out their adversaries. And the righteous shall see and be thankful, And rejoice with joy forever and ever, and shall see all their judgments and all their curses on their enemies.

(Jubilees 23:31)
And their bones shall rest in the earth, and their spirits shall have much joy, and they shall know that it is the Lord Who executes judgment, and shows mercy to hundreds and thousands and to all that love Him

(Jubilees 23:31)
And do you, Moses, write down these words; for thus are they written, and they record on the heavenly tablets for a testimony for the generations forever.

(Jubilees 24:)
And it came to pass after the death of Abraham, that the Lord blessed Isaac his son, and he arose from Hebron and went and dwelt at the Well of the Vision in the first year of the third week of this jubilee, seven years.

(Jubilees 24:2)
And in the first year of the fourth week a famine began in the land, besides the first famine, which had been in the days of Abraham.

~ ~ ~

(Jasher 27:1)
And Esau at that time, after the death of Abraham, frequently went in the field to hunt.

(Jasher 27:2)
And Nimrod king of Babel, the same was Amraphel, also frequently went with his mighty men to hunt in the field, and to walk about with his men in the cool of the day.

(Jasher 27:3)
And Nimrod was observing Esau all the days, for a jealousy was formed in the heart of Nimrod against Esau all the days.

(Jasher 27:4)
And on a certain day Esau went in the field to hunt, and he found Nimrod walking in the wilderness with his two men.

(Jasher 27:5)
And all his mighty men and his people were with him in the wilderness, but they removed at a distance from him, and they went from him in different directions to hunt, and Esau concealed himself for Nimrod, and he lurked for him in the wilderness.

(Jasher 27:6)
And Nimrod and his men that were with him did not know him, and Nimrod and his men frequently walked about in the field at the cool of the day, and to know where his men were hunting in the field.

(Jasher 27:7)
And Nimrod and two of his men that were with him came to the place where they were, when Esau started suddenly from his lurking place, and drew his sword, and hurried and ran to Nimrod and cut off his head.

(Jasher 27:8)
And Esau fought a desperate fight with the two men that were with Nimrod, and when they called out to him, Esau turned to them and smote them to death with his sword.

(Jasher 27:9)
And all the mighty men of Nimrod, who had left him to go to

the wilderness, heard the cry at a distance, and they knew the voices of those two men, and they ran to know the cause of it, when they found their king and the two men that were with him lying dead in the wilderness.

(Jasher 27:10)
And when Esau saw the mighty men of Nimrod coming at a distance, he fled, and thereby escaped; and Esau took the valuable garments of Nimrod, which Nimrod's father had bequeathed to Nimrod, and with which Nimrod prevailed over the whole land, and he ran and concealed them in his house.

(Jasher 27:11...)
And Esau took those garments and ran into the city on account of Nimrod's men.

~ ~ ~

(Genesis 25:29) (...Jasher 27:11) (Jubilees 21:3...)
And Jacob sod lentil pottage: and Esau came from the field hungry, and he came to his father's house wearied and exhausted from fight, and he was ready to die through grief when he approached his brother Jacob and sat before him and he was faint:

(Genesis 25:30) (...Jubilees 21:3...)
And Esau said to Jacob his brother, Feed me, I pray, with that same red pottage; for I am faint: therefore was his name called Edom.

(Genesis 25:31) (...Jubilees 21:3)

And Jacob said, Sell me your birthright this day and I will give you bread, and also some of this lentil pottage.

(Jubilees 21:4)

And Esau said in his heart: I shall die; of what profit to me is this birthright?

(Genesis 25:32) (Jasher 27:12...) (Jubilees 24:5...)

And Esau said to his brother Jacob, Behold, I about to die this day: and what profit shall this birthright do to me? And he said to Jacob: I give it to you.

(Genesis 25:33) (...Jasher 27:12) (...Jubilees 24:5)

And Jacob acted wisely with Esau in this matter. And Jacob said, Swear to me this day; and he swore to him: and Esau sold his birthright to Jacob, for it was so brought about by the Lord.

(Genesis 25:34) (Jubilees 24:6)

Then Jacob gave his brother Esau bread and pottage of lentils; and he ate and drank till he was satisfied, and rose up, and went his way: thus Esau despised his birthright. For this reason, Esau's name was called Edom, on account of the red pottage which Jacob gave him for his birthright.

(Jubilees 24:7)

And Jacob became the elder, and Esau was brought down from his dignity.

(Jasher 27:13)

And Esau's portion in the cave of the field of Machpelah, which Abraham had bought from the children of Heth for the possession of a burial ground, Esau also sold to Jacob, and

Jacob bought all this from his brother Esau for value given.

(Jasher 27:14)
And Jacob wrote the whole of this in a book, and he testified the same with witnesses, and he sealed it, and the book remained in the hands of Jacob.

(Jasher 27:15)
And when Nimrod the son of Cush died, his men lifted him up and brought him in consternation, and buried him in his city, and all the days that Nimrod lived were two hundred and fifteen years and he died.

(Jasher 27:16)
And the days that Nimrod reigned upon the people of the land were one hundred and eighty-five years; and Nimrod died by the sword of Esau in shame and contempt, and the seed of Abraham caused his death as he had seen in his dream.

(Jasher 27:17)
And at the death of Nimrod his kingdom became divided into many divisions, and all those parts that Nimrod reigned over were restored to the respective kings of the land, who recovered them after the death of Nimrod, and all the people of the house of Nimrod were for a long time enslaved to all the other kings of the land.

Genesis: Chapter Twenty-Six

(Genesis 26:1...) (Jasher 28:1) (Jubilees 24:8...)

And in those days, after the death of Abraham, in that year the Lord brought a heavy famine in the land, beside the first famine that was in the days of Abraham. And while the famine was raging in the land of Canaan, Isaac rose up to go down to Egypt in the second year of this week, on account of the famine, as his father Abraham had done.

(Jasher 28:2)

And the Lord appeared that night to Isaac and he said to him, Do not go down to Egypt but rise and go to Gerar, to Abimelech king of the Philistines, and remain there till the famine shall cease.

(...Genesis 26:1) (Jasher 28:3) (...Jubilees 24:8)

And Isaac rose up and went to Abimelech king of the Philistines to Gerar, as the Lord commanded him, and he remained there a full year.

(Genesis 26:2) (Jubilees 24:9...)

And the LORD appeared to him, and said to him, Do not go down into Egypt; dwell in the land of which I shall tell you:

(Genesis 26:3) (...Jubilees 24:9, 10...)

Sojourn in this land, and I will be with you, and will bless you; for to you, and to your seed, I will give all these countries, and I will perform the oath which I swore to Abraham your father;

(Genesis 26:4) (...Jubilees 24:10, 11...)
And I will make your seed to multiply as the stars of heaven, and will give to your seed all these countries; and in your seed, all the nations of the earth shall be blessed;

(Genesis 26:5) (...Jubilees 24:11)
Because that your father Abraham obeyed my voice, and kept my charge, my commandments, my statutes, and my laws and My covenant; and now obey My voice and dwell in this land.

(Genesis 26:6) (Jubilees 24:12)
And Isaac dwelt in Gerar three weeks of years.

(Genesis 26:7) (Jasher 28:4)
And when Isaac came to Gerar, the people of the land saw that Rebecca his wife was of a beautiful appearance, and the men of the place asked him of his wife; and he said, She is my sister: for he feared to say, She is my wife; lest, said he, the men of the place should kill me for Rebekah; because she was fair to look on.

(Jasher 28:5)
And the princes of Abimelech went and praised the woman to the king, but he answered them not, neither did he attend to their words.

(Jasher 28:6)
But he heard them say that Isaac declared her to be his sister, so the king reserved this within himself.

(Genesis 26:8) (Jasher 28:7)
And it came to pass, when he had been there a long time, when Isaac had remained three months in the land, that Abimelech king of the Philistines looked out at a window, and saw, and,

behold, Isaac was sporting with Rebekah his wife; for Isaac dwelt in the outer house belonging to the king, so that the house of Isaac was opposite the house of the king.

(Genesis 26:9) (Jasher 28:8..., 9)

And Abimelech the king called Isaac, and said to him, Behold, of a surety she is your wife: and why did you say, She is my sister? And Isaac said to him, Because I was afraid I said, Lest I die for her, therefore I said, She is my sister.

(Genesis 26:10) (...Jasher 28:8)

And Abimelech said, What is this you have done to us? One of the people might lightly have laid with your wife, and you would have brought guilt on us.

(Jasher 28:10)
At that time Abimelech gave orders to all his princes and great men, and they took Isaac and Rebecca his wife and brought them before the king.

(Genesis 26:11) (Jasher 28:11...) (Jubilees 24:13)

And the king commanded that they should dress them in princely garments, and make them ride through the streets of the city, and proclaim before them throughout the land, saying, This is the man and this is his wife; And Abimelech charged all his people concerning him, and concerning all that was his: He that touches this man or his wife shall surely be put to death.

(...Jasher 28:11)
And Isaac returned with his wife to the king's house, and the Lord was with Isaac and he continued to wax great and lacked nothing.

(Jasher 28:12)
And the Lord caused Isaac to find favor in the sight of Abimelech, and in the sight of all his subjects, and Abimelech acted well with Isaac, for Abimelech remembered the oath and the covenant that existed between his father and Abraham.

(Jasher 28:13)
And Abimelech said to Isaac, Behold the whole earth is before you; dwell wherever it may seem good in your sight until you shall return to your land; and Abimelech gave Isaac fields and vineyards and the best part of the land of Gerar, to sow and reap and eat the fruits of the ground until the days of the famine should have passed by.

(Genesis 26:12) (Jasher 28:14) (Jubilees 24:15...)
Then Isaac sowed in that land of the Philistines, and received in the same year a hundredfold: and the LORD blessed him.

(Genesis 26:13) (Jasher 28:15...) (Jubilees 24:14..., ...15...)
And the man waxed great among the Philistines, and went forward, and grew until he became very great:

(Genesis 26:14) (...Jasher 28:15) (...Jubilees 24:14, ...15)
For he had possession of flocks, and possession of herds, and great store of servants: he got many possessions, oxen and sheep and camels and donkeys and a great household, and the Philistines envied him.

(Genesis 26:15) (Jubilees 24:16)
For all the wells which his father's servants had dug in the days of Abraham his father, the Philistines had stopped them, after the death of Abraham, and filled them with earth.

(Genesis 26:16) (Jubilees 24:17...)

And Abimelech said to Isaac, Go from us; for you are much mightier than we.

(Genesis 26:17) (Jasher 28:16) (...Jubilees 24:17)

And when the days of the famine had passed away the Lord appeared to Isaac and said to him, Rise up, go forth from this place and return to your land, to the land of Canaan; And Isaac rose up and departed there, in the first year of the seventh week, and returned to Hebron which is in the land of Canaan, he and all belonging to him as the Lord commanded him, and pitched his tent and sojourned in the valley of Gerar, and dwelt there.

(Jasher 28:17)

And after this Shelach the son at Arpachshad died in that year, which is the eighteenth year of the lives of Jacob and Esau; and all the days that Shelach lived were four hundred and thirty-three years and he died.

(Jasher 28:18)

At that time Isaac sent his younger son Jacob to the house of Shem and Eber, and he learned the instructions of the Lord, and Jacob remained in the house of Shem and Eber for thirty-two years, and Esau his brother did not go, for he was not willing to go, and he remained in his father's house in the land of Canaan.

(Genesis 26:18) (Jubilees 24:18)

And Isaac dug again the wells of water, which the servants of Abraham, his father, had dug, in the days of Abraham his father; for the Philistines had stopped them after the death of Abraham his father: and he called their names after the names by which Abraham his father had called them.

(Genesis 26:19) (Jubilees 24:19...)

And Isaac's servants dug a well in the valley, and found there a well of springing water.

(Genesis 26:20) (...Jubilees 24:19)

And the herdsmen of Gerar strove with Isaac's herdsmen, saying, The water is ours: and Isaac called the name of the well Esek, Perversity; because they strove with him and had been perverse with us.

(Genesis 26:21) (Jubilees 24:20...)

And they dug another well, and strove for that also: and he called the name of it Sitnah, Enmity.

(Genesis 26:22) (...Jubilees 24:20)

And he removed from there, and dug another well; and for that they did not strive: and he called the name of it Rehoboth, Room; and he said, For now, the LORD has made room for us, and we shall be fruitful in the land.

(Genesis 26:23) (Jubilees 24:21)

And he went up from there to Beersheba, the Well of the Oath, in the first year of the first week in the forty-fourth jubilee.

(Genesis 26:24) (Jubilees 24:22)

And the LORD appeared to him the same night, on the new moon of the first month, and said to him, I am the God of Abraham your father: fear not, for I am with you, and will bless you, and multiply your seed as the sand of the earth, for my servant Abraham's sake.

(Genesis 26:25) (Jubilees 24:23, 24)

And he built an altar there, which Abraham his father had first built, and called on the name of the LORD, and he offered sacrifice to the God of Abraham his father, and pitched his tent there: and there Isaac's servants dug a well, and they found living water.

(Genesis 26:26)
Then Abimelech went to him from Gerar, and Ahuzzath one of his friends, and Phichol the chief captain of his army.

(Genesis 26:27)
And Isaac said to them, Why do you come to me, seeing you hate me, and have sent me away from you?

(Genesis 26:28)
And they said, We saw certainly that the LORD was with you: and we said, Let there be now an oath between us, even between us and you, and let us make a covenant with you;

(Genesis 26:29)
That you will do us no hurt, as we have not touched you, and as we have done to you nothing but good, and have sent you away in peace: you are now the blessed of the LORD.

(Genesis 26:30)
And he made them a feast, and they ate and drink.

(Genesis 26:31)
And they rose up betimes in the morning, and swore one to another: and Isaac sent them away, and they departed from him in peace.

(Jubilees 24:25)
And the servants of Isaac dug another well and did not find water, and they went and told Isaac that they had not found water, and Isaac said: I have sworn this day to the Philistines

and this thing has been announced to us.

(Jubilees 24:26)
And he called the name of that place the Well of the Oath; for there he had sworn to Abimelech and Ahuzzath his friend and Phicol the prefect Or his host.

(Jubilees 24:27)
And Isaac knew that day that under constraint he had sworn to them to make peace with them.

(Jubilees 24:28)
And Isaac on that day cursed the Philistines and said: Cursed be the Philistines to the day of wrath and indignation from the midst of all nations; may God make them a derision and a curse and an object of wrath and indignation in the hands of the sinners the Gentiles and in the hands of the Kittim.

(Jubilees 24:29)
And whoever escapes the sword of the enemy and the Kittim, may the righteous nation root out in judgment from under heaven; for they shall be the enemies and foes of my children throughout their generations on the earth.

(Jubilees 24:30)
And no remnant shall be left to them, nor one that shall be saved on the day of the wrath of judgment; for destruction and rooting out and expulsion from the earth is the whole seed of the Philistines. And there shall no longer be left for these Caphtorim a name or a seed on the earth.

(Jubilees 24:31)
For though he ascend to heaven, there shall he be brought down, and though he make himself strong on earth, There

shall he be dragged forth, and though he hide himself among the nations, even from there shall he be rooted out; and though he descend into Sheol, There also shall his condemnation be great, and there also he shall have no peace.

(Jubilees 24:32)
And if he go into captivity, by the hands of those that seek his life shall they slay him on the way, and neither name nor seed shall be left to him on all the earth; for into eternal malediction shall he depart.

(Jubilees 24:33)
And thus is it written and engraved concerning him on the heavenly tablets, to do to him on the day of judgment, so that he may be rooted out of the earth.

(Genesis 26:32)

And it came to pass the same day, that Isaac's servants came, and told him concerning the well which they had dug, and said to him, We have found water.

(Genesis 26:33)

And he called it Shebah: therefore, the name of the city is Beersheba to this day.

~ ~ ~

(Jasher 28:19)
And Esau was continually hunting in the fields to bring home what he could get, so did Esau all the days.

(Jasher 28:20)
And Esau was a designing and deceitful man, one who hunted after the hearts of men and inveigled them, and Esau was a valiant man in the field, and in the course of time went as usual to hunt; and he came as far as the field of Seir, the same is Edom.

(Jasher 28:21)
And he remained in the land of Seir hunting in the field a year and four months.

(Jasher 28:22)
And Esau there saw in the land of Seir the daughter of a man of Canaan, and her name was Jehudith, the daughter of Beeri, son of Epher, from the families of Heth the son of Canaan.

(Genesis 26:34) (Jasher 28:23)
And Esau was forty years old when he took to wife Judith the daughter of Beeri the Hittite, and Bashemath the daughter of Elon the Hittite: and he came to her; and he brought her to Hebron, the land of his father's dwelling place, and he dwelt there.

(Genesis 26:35)
Which were a grief of mind to Isaac and to Rebekah.

(Jubilees 25:1)
And in the second year of this week in this jubilee, Rebecca called Jacob her son, and spoke to him, saying: My son, do not take you a wife of the daughters of Canaan, as Esau, your brother, who took him two wives of the daughters of Canaan, and they have embittered my soul with all their unclean deeds: for all their deeds are fornication and lust, and there is no righteousness with them, for their deeds are evil.

(Jubilees 25:2)
And I, my son, love you exceedingly, and my heart and my affection bless you every hour of the day and watch of the night.

(Jubilees 25:3)
And now, my son, hearken to my voice, and do the will of your mother, and do not take you a wife of the daughters of this land, but only of the house of my father, and of my father's kindred. You shall take you a wife of the house of my father, and the Most High God will bless you, and your children shall be a righteous generation and a holy seed.

(Jubilees 25:4)
And then spoke Jacob to Rebecca, his mother, and said to her: Behold, mother, I am nine weeks of years old, and I neither know nor have I touched any woman, nor have I betrothed myself to any, nor even think of taking me a wife of the daughters of Canaan.

(Jubilees 25:5)
For I remember, mother, the words of Abraham, our father, for he commanded me not to take a wife of the daughters of Canaan, but to take me a wife from the seed of my father's house and from my kindred.

(Jubilees 25:6)
I have heard before that daughters have been born to Laban, your brother, and I have set my heart on them to take a wife from among them.

(Jubilees 25:7)
And for this reason, I have guarded myself in my spirit against sinning or being corrupted in all my ways throughout

all the days of my life; for with regard to lust and fornication, Abraham, my father, gave me many commands.

(Jubilees 25:8)
And, despite all that he has commanded me, these two and twenty years my brother has striven with me, and spoken frequently to me and said: My brother, take to wife a sister of my two wives; but I refuse to do as he has done.

(Jubilees 25:9)
I swear before you, mother, that all the days of my life I will not take me a wife from the daughters of the seed of Canaan, and I will not act wickedly as my brother has done.

(Jubilees 25:10)
Fear not, mother; be assured that I shall do your will and walk in uprightness, and not corrupt my ways forever.

(Jubilees 25:11)
And thereupon she lifted up her face to heaven and extended the fingers of her hands, and opened her mouth and blessed the Most High God, who had created the heaven and the earth, and she gave Him thanks and praise.

(Jubilees 25:12)
And she said: Blessed be the Lord God, and may His holy name be blessed forever and ever, Who has given me Jacob as a pure son and a holy seed; for he is Yours, and his seed shall be Yours continually and throughout all the generations forevermore.

(Jubilees 25:13)
Bless him, O Lord, and place in my mouth the blessing of righteousness, that I may bless him.

(Jubilees 25:14)
And at that hour, when the spirit of righteousness descended into her mouth, she placed both her hands on the head of Jacob, and said:

(Jubilees 25:15)
Blessed are you, Lord of righteousness and God of the ages and may He bless You beyond all the generations of men. May He give you, my son, the path of righteousness, and reveal righteousness to your seed.

(Jubilees 25:16)
And may He make your sons many during your life, and may they arise according to the number of the months of the year. And may their sons become many and great beyond the stars of heaven, and their numbers be more than the sand of the sea.

(Jubilees 25:17)
And may He give them this goodly land as He said He would give it to Abraham and to his seed after him always-and may they hold it as a possession forever.

(Jubilees 25:18)
And may I see born to you, my son, blessed children during my life, and a blessed and holy seed may all your seed be.

(Jubilees 25:19)
And as you have refreshed your mother's spirit during her life, the womb of her that bare you blesses you thus,My affection and my breasts bless you and my mouth and my tongue praise you greatly.

(Jubilees 25:20)
Increase and spread over the earth, and may your seed be perfect in the joy of heaven and earth forever; and may your seed rejoice, and on the great day of peace may it have peace.

(Jubilees 25:21)
And may your name and your seed endure to all the ages, and may the Most High God be their God, and may the God of righteousness dwell with them, and by them may His sanctuary be built to all the ages.

(Jubilees 25:22)
Blessed be he that blesses you, and all flesh that curses you falsely, may it be cursed.

(Jubilees 25:23)
And she kissed him, and said to him; May the Lord of the world love you as the heart of your mother and her affection rejoice in you and bless you. And she ceased from blessing.

~ ~ ~

(Jasher 28:24)
And it came to pass in those days, in the hundred and tenth year of the life of Isaac, that is in the fiftieth year of the life of Jacob, in that year died Shem, the son of Noah; Shem was six hundred years old at his death.

(Jasher 28:25)
And when Shem died Jacob returned to his father to Hebron which is in the land of Canaan.

(Jasher 28:26)
And in the fifty-sixth year of the life of Jacob, people came from Haran, and Rebecca was told concerning her brother Laban the son of Bethuel.

(Jasher 28:27)
For the wife of Laban was barren in those days, and bare no children, and also all his handmaids bare none to him.

(Jasher 28:28)
And the Lord afterward remembered Adinah the wife of Laban, and she conceived and bare twin daughters, and Laban called the names of his daughters, the name of the elder Leah, and the name of the younger Rachel.

(Jasher 28:29)
And those people came and told these things to Rebecca, and Rebecca rejoiced greatly that the Lord had visited her brother and that he had got children.

Genesis: Chapter Twenty-Seven

(Genesis 27:1) (Jasher 29:1, 2...) (Jubilees 26:1...)

And in the seventh year of this week, it came to pass, that when Isaac was old, and advanced in days, and his eyes became heavy through age; they were dim, so that he could not see, he called Esau his eldest son, and said to him, My son: and he said to him, Behold, here am I.

(Genesis 27:2) (...Jasher 29:2...) (...Jubilees 26:1)

And he said, Behold now, I am old, and gray-headed; and behold my eyes are dim in seeing, I know not the day of my death:

(Genesis 27:3) (...Jasher 29:2...) (Jubilees 26:2...)

Now therefore take, I pray, your weapons, your quiver and your bow, rise up and go out to the field, and take me some venison, my son;

(Genesis 27:4) (...Jasher 29:2) (...Jubilees 26:2)

And make me savory meat, such as I love, and bring it to me, that I may eat; that my soul may bless you before I die.

(Genesis 27:5) (Jasher 29:3, 4...) (Jubilees 26:3, 4)

And Rebekah heard all the words when Isaac spoke to Esau his son. And Esau took his weapon and went forth early to the field to hunt for venison, as usual, and to bring it to his father as he had ordered him, so that he might bless him.

(Genesis 27:6) (...Jasher 29:4...) (Jubilees 26:5...)

And Rebekah hurried and spoke to Jacob her son, saying,

Behold, I heard Isaac your father speak to Esau your brother, saying,

(Genesis 27:7) (...Jubilees 26:5, 6...)
Hunt for me, and bring me venison, and make me savory meat, and bring it to me that I may eat, and bless you before the LORD before my death.

(Genesis 27:8) (...Jasher 29:4) (...Jubilees 26:6...)
Now therefore, my son, obey my voice and hasten and make according to that which I command you.

(Genesis 27:9) (Jasher 29:5...) (...Jubilees 26:6...)
Go now to the flock, and fetch me from there two good kids of the goats; and I will make them savory meat for your father, such as he loves:

(Genesis 27:10) (...Jasher 29:5) (...Jubilees 26:6)
And you shall bring it to your father, that he may eat before your brother shall have come from the chase, and that he may bless you before the Lord before his death and that you may be blessed.

(Jubilees 26:7)
And Jacob said to Rebecca his mother: Mother, I shall not withhold anything which my father would eat, and which would please him: only I fear, my mother, that he will recognize my voice and wish to touch me.

(Genesis 27:11) (Jubilees 26:8...)
And Jacob said to Rebekah his mother, Behold, Esau my brother is a hairy man, and you know that I am a smooth man:

(Genesis 27:12) (...Jubilees 26:8)
My father peradventure will feel me, and I shall seem to him as a deceiver; and shall do a deed which he had not commanded me, and he will be mad at me, and I shall bring a curse on me, and not a blessing.

(Genesis 27:13) (Jubilees 26:9)
And Rebecca his mother said to him, your curse be on me, my son: only obey my voice, and go fetch me them.

(Genesis 27:14) (Jasher 29:6...) (Jubilees 26:10)
And Jacob obeyed the voice of Rebecca, his mother. And he went and did, and fetched two good and fat kids of the goats, and brought them to his mother as his mother had commanded him: and his mother made savory meat, such as his father loved.

(Genesis 27:15) (Jubilees 26:11...)
And Rebekah took goodly raiment of her eldest son Esau, which were with her in the house, and put them on Jacob her younger son:

(Genesis 27:16) (...Jubilees 26:11)
And she put the skins of the kids of the goats on his hands, and on the smooth, exposed parts of his neck:

(Genesis 27:17) (Jubilees 26:12)
And she gave the savory meat and the bread, which she had prepared, into the hand of her son Jacob.

(Genesis 27:18) (...Jasher 29:6, 7...) (Jubilees 26:13...)
And he came to and brought it before to his father before Esau had come from his chase, and said, My father: and he said to Jacob, Here am I; who are you, my son?

(Genesis 27:19) (...Jasher 29:7) (...Jubilees 26:13)
And Jacob said to his father, I am Esau your firstborn; I have done according as you asked me: now therefore arise, I pray, sit and eat of my venison, which I have caught, father, that your soul may bless me as you spoke to me.

(Genesis 27:20) (Jubilees 26:14, 15)
And Isaac said to his son, How did you find it so quickly, my son? And he said, Because the LORD your God brought it to me and caused me to find it.

(Genesis 27:21) (Jubilees 26:16)
And Isaac said to Jacob, Come near, I pray, that I may feel you, my son, whether you be my very son Esau or not.

(Genesis 27:22) (Jubilees 26:17)
And Jacob went near to Isaac his father; and he felt him, and said, The voice is Jacob's voice, but the hands are the hands of Esau.

(Genesis 27:23) (Jubilees 26:18)
And he did not discern him, because it was a dispensation from heaven to remove his power of perception and Isaac discerned not, for his hands were hairy, as his brother Esau's hands: so he blessed him.

(Genesis 27:24) (Jubilees 26:19...)
And he said, Are you my very son Esau? And he said, I am your son.

(Genesis 27:25) (Jasher 29:8...) (...Jubilees 26:19, 20)
And he said, Bring it near to me, and I will eat of my son's venison, of that which you have caught, my son, that my soul may bless you. And he brought it near to him. And Isaac rose

up and he ate: and he brought him wine, and he drank and his heart was comforted.

(Genesis 27:26) (Jubilees 26:21)
And his father Isaac said to him, Come near now, and kiss me, my son.

(Genesis 27:27) (...Jasher 29:8...) (Jubilees 26:22)
And he came near, and kissed him: and he smelled the smell of his raiment, and he blessed Jacob, and said, See, the smell of my son is as the smell of a field which the LORD has blessed:

(Genesis 27:28) (Jubilees 26:23...)
Therefore, God give you of the dew of heaven, and the fatness of the earth, and plenty of corn and wine:

(Genesis 27:29) (...Jubilees 26:23, 24)
Let people serve you, and nations bow down to you: be lord over your brethren, and let your mother's sons bow down to you: and may all the blessings wherewith the Lord has blessed me and blessed Abraham, my father; be imparted to you and to your seed forever: cursed be every one that curses you, and blessed be he that blesses you.

(Genesis 27:30) (...Jasher 29:8...) (Jubilees 26:25)
And Jacob went away from his father; it came to pass, as soon as Isaac had made an end of blessing Jacob, and Jacob was yet scarce gone out from the presence of Isaac his father, he hid himself and Esau his brother came in from his hunting from the field.

(Genesis 27:31) (...Jasher 29:8) (Jubilees 26:26)
And he also had made savory meat, and brought it to his father to eat thereof and to bless him, and said to his father,

Let my father arise, and eat of his son's venison, that your soul may bless me.

(Genesis 27:32) (Jubilees 26:27)

And Isaac his father said to him, Who are you? And he said, I am your son, your firstborn Esau. I have done as you have commanded me.

(Genesis 27:33) (Jasher 29:9...) (Jubilees 26:28)

And Isaac was very greatly astonished and trembled very exceedingly, and Isaac said to Esau, Who? Where is he that has taken venison, and brought it me, and I have eaten of all before you came, and have blessed him? Yea, and he shall be blessed and all his seed forever.

(Genesis 27:34) (Jasher 29:10...) (Jubilees 26:29)

And it came to pass when Esau heard the words of his father Isaac, he cried with a great and exceeding bitter cry, and said to his father, Bless me, even me also, O my father.

(...Jasher 29:9)

And Esau knew that his brother Jacob had done this, and the anger of Esau was kindled against his brother Jacob that he had acted thus toward him.

(Genesis 27:35) (...Jasher 29:10...) (Jubilees 26:30...)

And when Isaac heard the voice of his son Esau weeping, Isaac said to Esau, What can I do, my son, your brother came subtly, and has taken away your blessing.

(Genesis 27:36) (...Jasher 29:10...) (...Jubilees 26:30, 31...)

And Esau said, Is not he rightly named Jacob? For he has supplanted me these two times: he took away my birthright; and, behold, now he has taken away my blessing. And he said,

Have you not reserved a blessing for me, father?

(Genesis 27:37) (...Jubilees 26:31)
And Isaac answered and said to Esau, Behold, I have made him your lord, and all his brethren have I given to him for servants; and with plenty of corn and wine and oil have I sustained him: and what shall I do now to you, my son?

(Genesis 27:38) (Jubilees 26:32. 33...)
And Esau said to Isaac, his father, Do you only have one blessing, my father? Bless me, even me also, O my father. And Esau lifted up his voice, and wept.

(Genesis 27:39) (...Jubilees 26:33)
And Isaac his father answered and said to him, Behold, your dwelling shall be far from the fatness of the earth, and far from the dew of heaven from above;

(Genesis 27:40) (Jubilees 26:34)
And by your sword shall you live, and shall serve your brother; and it shall come to pass when you shall have the dominion, that you shall break his yoke from off your neck. You shall sin a complete sin to death, and your seed shall be rooted out from under heaven.

(Genesis 27:41) (...Jasher 29:10) (Jubilees 26:35)
And Esau kept threatening Jacob. And Esau hated his brother Jacob because of the blessing wherewith his father blessed him: and his anger was greatly roused against him and Esau said in his heart, The days of mourning for my father are at hand; then will I slay my brother Jacob.

(Jasher 29:11)
And Jacob was very much afraid of his brother Esau, and he

rose up and fled to the house of Eber the son of Shem, and he concealed himself there on account of his brother, and Jacob was sixty-three years old when he went forth from the land of Canaan from Hebron, and Jacob was concealed in Eber's house fourteen years on account of his brother Esau, and he there continued to learn the ways of the Lord and his commandments.

(Jasher 29:12)
And when Esau saw that Jacob had fled and escaped from him, and that Jacob had cunningly obtained the blessing, then Esau grieved exceedingly, and he was also vexed at his father and mother; and he also rose up and took his wife and went away from his father and mother to the land of Seir, and he dwelt there; and Esau saw there a woman from among the daughters of Heth whose name was Bosmath, the daughter of Elon the Hittite, and he took her for a wife in addition to his first wife, and Esau called her name Adah, saying the blessing had in that time passed from him.

(Jasher 29:13)
And Esau dwelt in the land of Seir six months without seeing his father and mother, and afterward Esau took his wives and rose up and returned to the land of Canaan, and Esau placed his two wives in his father's house in Hebron.

(Jasher 29:14)
And the wives of Esau vexed and provoked Isaac and Rebecca with their works, for they walked not in the ways of the Lord, but served their father's gods of wood and stone as their father had taught them, and they were more wicked than their father.

(Jasher 29:15)
And they went according to the evil desires of their hearts,

and they sacrificed and burnt incense to the Baalim, and Isaac and Rebecca became weary of them.

(Jasher 29:20)
And at the end of fourteen years of Jacob's residing in the house of Eber, Jacob desired to see his father and mother, and Jacob came to the house of his father and mother to Hebron, and Esau had in those days forgotten what Jacob had done to him in having taken the blessing from him in those days.

(Jasher 29:21)
And when Esau saw Jacob coming to his father and mother he remembered what Jacob had done to him, and he was greatly incensed against him and he sought to slay him.

(Jasher 29:21)
And Isaac the son of Abraham was old and advanced in days, and Esau said, Now my father's time is drawing nigh that he must die, and when he shall die I will slay my brother Jacob.

(Genesis 27:42) (Jasher 29:23...) (Jubilees 27:1, 2)
And these words of Esau her elder son were told to Rebekah in a dream: and she sent and called Jacob her younger son, and said to him, Behold, your brother Esau, will take vengeance on you, and he comforts himself, purposing to kill you.

(Genesis 27:43) (...Jasher 29:23...) (Jubilees 27:3...)
Now therefore, my son, obey my voice; and arise, flee you to Laban my brother to Haran;

(Genesis 27:44) (...Jasher 29:23) (...Jubilees 27:3...)
And tarry with him a few days, until your brother's fury turn away; and then shall you come back.

(Genesis 27:45...) (...Jubilees 27:3)

Until your brother's anger turn away from you, and he forget that which you have done to him: then I will send, and fetch you from there:

(Jubilees 27:4)

And Jacob said: I am not afraid; if he wishes to kill me, I will kill him.

(...Genesis 27:45) (Jubilees 27:5)

But she said to him: Let me not be bereft of both my sons on one day. Why should I be deprived also of you both in one day?

(Jubilees 27:6)

And Jacob said to Rebecca his mother: Behold, you know that my father has become old, and does not see because his eyes are dull, and if I leave him it will be evil in his eyes, because I leave him and go away from you, and my father will be angry, and will curse me. I will not go; when he sends me, then only will I go.

(Jubilees 27:7)

And Rebecca said to Jacob: I will go in and speak to him, and he will send you away.

(Genesis 27:46) (Jasher 29:16) (Jubilees 27:8)

And Rebekah said to Isaac, I am weary of my life because of the daughters of Heth, whom Esau has taken him as wives; if Jacob take a wife of the daughters of Heth, such as these which are of the daughters of the land, what good shall my life do me? For the daughters of Canaan are evil.

(Jasher 29:17)
And in those days Adah the wife of Esau conceived and bare him a son, and Esau called the name of the son that was born to him Eliphaz, and Esau was sixty-five years old when she bare him.

(Jasher 29:18)
And Ishmael the son of Abraham died in those days, in the sixty-forth year of the life of Jacob, and all the days that Ishmael lived were one hundred and thirty-seven years and he died.

(Jasher 29:19)
And when Isaac heard that Ishmael was dead he mourned for him, and Isaac lamented over him many days.

Genesis: Chapter Twenty-Eight

(Genesis 28:1) (Jasher 29:24) (Jubilees 27:9)

And Isaac called Jacob, and blessed him, and charged him, and said to him, You shall not take a wife of the daughters of Canaan; for thus our father Abraham commanded us according to the word of the Lord which he had commanded him, saying, To your seed will I give this land; if your children keep my covenant that I have made with you, then will I also perform to your children that which I have spoken to you and I will not forsake them.

(Genesis 28:2) (Jasher 29:25) (Jubilees 27:10)

Now therefore my son hearken to my voice, to all that I shall command you, and refrain from taking a wife from among the daughters of Canaan; arise, go to Mesopotamia, to Padanaram (Haran), to the house of Bethuel your mother's father; and take you a wife from there of the daughters of Laban your mother's brother.

(Jasher 29:26)

Therefore, take heed lest you should forget the Lord your God and all his ways in the land to which you go, and should get connected with the people of the land and pursue vanity and forsake the Lord your God.

(Jasher 29:27)

But when you come to the land serve there the Lord, do not turn to the right or to the left from the way which I commanded you and which you learned.

(Jasher 29:28)
And may the Almighty God grant you favor in the sight of the people of the earth, that you mayest take there a wife according to your choice; one who is good and upright in the ways of the Lord.

(Genesis 28:3) (Jasher 29:29...) (Jubilees 27:11...)
And may God Almighty bless you, and make you fruitful, and multiply you, that you may be a multitude of people in the land whither you go, and may God cause you to return to this land, the land of your father's dwelling, with children and with great riches, with joy and with pleasure.

(Genesis 28:4) (...Jasher 29:29) (...Jubilees 27:11)
And give you the blessing of Abraham, to you, and to your seed with you; that you may inherit the land wherein you are a stranger, which God gave to Abraham. Go, my son, in peace.

(Genesis 28:5) (...Jasher 29:30) (Jubilees 27:12)
And Isaac finished commanding Jacob and blessing him, and he gave him many gifts, together with silver and gold, and he sent away Jacob: and Jacob hearkened to his father and mother; he kissed them and arose and he went to Mesopotamia, to Padanaram to Laban, son of Bethuel the Syrian, the brother of Rebekah, Jacob's and Esau's mother. And Jacob was seventy seven years old when he went out from the land of Canaan from Beersheba.

(Jubilees 27:13)
And it came to pass after Jacob had arisen to go to Mesopotamia that the spirit of Rebecca was grieved after her son, and she wept.

(Jubilees 27:14)
And Isaac said to Rebecca: My sister, do not weep on account of Jacob, my son; for he goes in peace, and in peace will he return.

(Jubilees 27:15)
The Most High God will preserve him from all evil, and will be with him; for He will not forsake him all his days;

(Jubilees 27:16)
For I know that his ways will be prospered in all things wherever he goes, until he return in peace to us, and we see him in peace.

(Jubilees 27:17)
Fear not on his account, my sister, for he is on the upright path and he is a perfect man: and he is faithful and will not perish. Weep not.

(Jubilees 27:18)
And Isaac comforted Rebecca on account of her son Jacob, and blessed him.

(Genesis 28:6)
When Esau saw that Isaac had blessed Jacob, and sent him away to Padanaram, to take him a wife from there; and that as he blessed him he gave him a charge, saying, You shall not take a wife of the daughters of Canaan;

(Genesis 28:7)
And that Jacob obeyed his father and his mother, and was gone to Padanaram;

(Jasher 29:31)
And when Jacob went away to go to Haran, Esau called to his son Eliphaz, and secretly spoke to him, saying, Now hurry, take your sword in your hand and pursue Jacob and pass before him in the road, and lurk for him, and slay him with your sword in one of the mountains, and take all belonging to him and come back.

(Jasher 29:32)
And Eliphaz the son of Esau was an active man and expert with the bow as his father had taught him, and he was a noted hunter in the field and a valiant man.

(Jasher 29:33)
And Eliphaz did as his father had commanded him, and Eliphaz was at that time thirteen years old, and Eliphaz rose up and went and took ten of his mother's brothers with him and pursued Jacob.

(Jasher 29:34)
And he closely followed Jacob, and he lurked for him in the border of the land of Canaan opposite to the city of Shechem.

(Jasher 29:35)
And Jacob saw Eliphaz and his men pursuing him, and Jacob stood still in the place in which he was going, in order to know what this was, for he did not know the thing; and Eliphaz drew his sword and he went on advancing, he and his men, toward Jacob; and Jacob said to them, What is to do with you that you have come hither, and what does it mean that you pursue with your swords.

(Jasher 29:36)
And Eliphaz came near to Jacob and he answered and said to

him, Thus, my father commanded me, and now therefore I will not deviate from the orders which my father gave me; and when Jacob saw that Esau had spoken to Eliphaz to employ force, Jacob then approached and supplicated Eliphaz and his men, saying to him,

(Jasher 29:37)
Behold all that I have and which my father and mother gave to me, that take to you and go from me, and do not slay me, and may this thing be accounted to you a righteousness.

(Jasher 29:38)
And the Lord caused Jacob to find favor in the sight of Eliphaz the son of Esau, and his men, and they hearkened to the voice of Jacob, and they did not put him to death, and Eliphaz and his men took all belonging to Jacob together with the silver and gold that he had brought with him from Beersheba; they left him nothing.

(Jasher 29:39)
And Eliphaz and his men went away from him and they returned to Esau to Beersheba, and they told him all that had occurred to them with Jacob, and they gave him all that they had taken from Jacob.

(Jasher 29:40)
And Esau was indignant at Eliphaz his son, and at his men that were with him, because they had not put Jacob to death.

(Jasher 29:41)
And they answered and said to Esau, Because Jacob supplicated us in this matter not to slay him, our pity was excited toward him, and we took all belonging to him and brought it to you; and Esau took all the silver and gold which Eliphaz had taken

from Jacob and he put them by in his house.

(Genesis 28:8) (Jasher 29:42)

At that time when Esau saw that Isaac had blessed Jacob, and had commanded him, saying, You shall not take a wife from among the daughters of Canaan, and that the daughters of Canaan did not please Isaac his father and Rebecca;

(Genesis 28:9) (Jasher 29:43)

Then went Esau to the house of Ishmael his uncle, and took to the wives which he had Mahalath the daughter of Ishmael Abraham's son, the sister of Nebajoth, to be his wife.

(Genesis 28:10) (Jasher 30:1...) (Jubilees 27:19...)

And Jacob went from the Well of the Oath, out from Beersheba, and went toward Haran, on the first year of the second week in the forty-fourth jubilee, and he came as far as mount Moriah.

(Genesis 28:11) (...Jasher 30:1...) (...Jubilees 27:19, 20...)

And he lighted on a certain place, and tarried there all night, near the city of Luz, on the mountains, that is, Bethel, on the new moon of the first month of this week, and he came to the place at even and turned from the way to the west of the road that night: and he slept there; because the sun was set; and he took of the stones of that place, and laid and put them for his pillows, under the tree, and he was journeying alone, and lay down in that place to sleep.

(Genesis 28:12) (...Jubilees 27: 20, 21...)

And he slept. And he dreamed that night, and behold a ladder set up on the earth, and the top of it reached to heaven: and behold the angels of God ascending and descending on it.

(Genesis 28:13) (...Jasher 30:1) (...Jubilees 27: 21, 22)
And, behold, the Lord appeared there to Jacob on that night. The LORD stood above the ladder, and He said to him, I am the LORD God of Abraham your father, and the God of Isaac your father; the land you are laying on, I give it to you, and to your seed after you;

(Genesis 28:14) (Jubilees 27:23)
And your seed shall be as the dust of the earth, and you shall spread abroad to the west, and to the east, and to the north, and to the south: and in you and in your seed shall all the families of the earth be blessed.

(Genesis 28:15) (Jasher 30:2) (Jubilees 27:24)
And, behold, I am with you, and will keep you in all places where you go, and I will multiply your seed as the stars of Heaven, and I will cause all your enemies to fall before you; and when they shall make war with you they shall not prevail over you, and I will bring you again into this land with joy, with children, and with great riches; for I will not leave you, until I have done that which I have spoken to you of.

(Genesis 28:16) (Jasher 30:3...) (Jubilees 27: 25...)
And Jacob awoke out of his sleep, and he rejoiced greatly at the vision which he had seen; and he said, Surely the LORD is in this place; and I did not know it.

(Genesis 28:17) (...Jubilees 27: 25)
And he was afraid, and said, How dreadful is this place! This is none other but the house of God, and this is the gate of heaven.

(Genesis 28:18) (Jubilees 27: 26...)
And Jacob rose up early in the morning, and took the stone

that he had put for his pillows, and set it up for a pillar for a sign, and poured oil on the top of it.

(Genesis 28:19) (...Jasher 30:3) (...Jubilees 27: 26)
And he called the name of that place Bethel: but the name of that city was called Luz at the first.

(Genesis 28:20) (Jubilees 27: 27...)
And Jacob vowed a vow, saying, If God will be with me, and will keep me in this way that I go, and will give me bread to eat, and raiment to put on,

(Genesis 28:21) (...Jubilees 27: 27...)
So that I come again to my father's house in peace; then shall the LORD be My God:

(Genesis 28:22) (...Jubilees 27: 27)
And this stone, which I have set for a pillar, for a sign in this place, shall be God's house: and of all that You shall give me I will surely give the tenth to You.

(Jasher 30:4...)
And Jacob rose up from that place quite rejoiced, and when he walked his feet felt light to him for joy.

Genesis: Chapter Twenty-Nine

(Genesis 29:1) (...Jasher 30:4...) (Jubilees 28:1...)
Then Jacob went from there on his journey, and came into the land of the people of the east, to Laban, the brother of Rebecca.

(Genesis 29:2) (...Jasher 30:4)
And he returned to Haran. And he looked, and behold a well in the field, and, lo, there were three flocks of sheep lying by it; for out of that well they watered the flocks: and a great stone was on the well's mouth, and he set by the shepherd's well.

(Genesis 29:3)
And there all were the flocks gathered: and they rolled the stone from the well's mouth, and watered the sheep, and put the stone again on the well's mouth in his place.

(Jasher 30:5)
And he there found some men; going from Haran to feed their flocks, and Jacob made inquiries of them, and they said, We are from Haran.

(Genesis 29:4)
And Jacob said to them, My brethren, where are you from? And they said, We are from Haran.

(Genesis 29:5) (Jasher 30:6...)
And he said to them, Do you know Laban the son of Nahor? And they said, We know him.

(Genesis 29:6) (...Jasher 30:6)

And he said to them, Is he well? And they said, He is well: and, behold, Rachel his daughter comes with the sheep, to feed her father's flock.

(Genesis 29:7)

And he said, Lo, it is yet high day, neither is it time that the cattle should be gathered together: water the sheep, and go and feed them.

(Genesis 29:8)

And they said, We cannot, until all the flocks be gathered together, and till they roll the stone from the well's mouth; then we will water the sheep.

(Genesis 29:9) (Jasher 30:7)

And while he yet spoke with them, Rachel the daughter of Laban came with her father's sheep: for she kept them.

(Genesis 29:10) (Jasher 30:8...)

And it came to pass, when Jacob saw Rachel the daughter of Laban his mother's brother, and the sheep of Laban his mother's brother, that Jacob went near, and rolled the stone from the well's mouth, and watered the flock of Laban his mother's brother.

(Genesis 29:11) (...Jasher 30:8)

And Jacob ran and kissed Rachel, and lifted up his voice, and wept.

(Genesis 29:12) (Jasher 30:9)

And Jacob told Rachel that he was her father's brother, and that he was Rebekah's son: and she ran and told her father, and Jacob continued to cry because he had nothing with him to bring to the house of Laban.

(Genesis 29:13) (Jasher 30:10, 11)
And it came to pass, when Laban heard the tidings of Jacob his sister's son, that he ran to meet him, and embraced him, and kissed him, and brought him to his house and gave him bread, and he ate. And he told Laban all these things, what his brother Esau had done to him, and what his son Eliphaz had done to him in the road.

(Genesis 29:14) (Jasher 30:12...) (...Jubilees 28:1...)
And Laban said to him, Surely you are my bone and my flesh. And he stayed with him the space of a month, and Jacob ate and drank in the house of Laban.

(Genesis 29:15) (...Jasher 30:12)
And Laban said to Jacob, Because you are my brother, should you therefore serve me for nothing? Tell me, what shall your wages be?

(Genesis 29:16) (Jasher 30:13...)
And Laban had no sons but only daughters, and his other wives and handmaids were still barren in those days; And Laban had two daughters: and these are the names of Laban's daughters which his wife Adinah had borne to him; the name of the elder was Leah, and the name of the younger was Rachel.

(Genesis 29:17) (...Jasher 30:13...) (Jubilees 28:5...)
Leah was tender and weak eyed but her form was very handsome; but Rachel had beautiful eyes and was beautiful and well favored, and very handsome form.

(Genesis 29:18) (...Jasher 30:13, 14...)

And Jacob loved Rachel; and Jacob said to Laban, I will serve you seven years for Rachel your younger daughter.

(Genesis 29:19) (...Jasher 30:14...)

And Laban consented and said, It is better that I give her to you, than that I should give her to another man: abide with me.

(Genesis 29:20) (...Jasher 30:14) (...Jubilees 28:1)

And Jacob served seven years (one week of years) for his daughter Rachel; and they seemed to him but a few days, for the love he had to her.

(Jasher 30:15)

And in the second year of Jacob's dwelling in Haran, that is in the seventy ninth year of the life of Jacob, in that year died Eber the son of Shem, he was four hundred and sixty- four years old at his death.

(Jasher 30:16)

And when Jacob heard that Eber was dead he grieved exceedingly, and he lamented and mourned over him many days.

(Jasher 30:17)

And in the third year of Jacob's dwelling in Haran, Bosmath, the daughter of Ishmael, the wife of Esau, bare to him a son, and Esau called his name Reuel.

(Jasher 30:18)

And in the fourth year of Jacob's residence in the house of Laban, the Lord visited Laban and remembered him on account of Jacob, and sons were born to him, and his first born was Beor, his second was Alib, and the third was Chorash.

(Jasher 30:19)
And the Lord gave Laban riches and honor, sons and daughters, and the man increased greatly on account of Jacob.

(Jasher 30:20)
And Jacob in those days served Laban in all manner of work, in the house and in the field, and the blessing of the Lord was in all that belonged to Laban in the house and in the field.

(Jasher 30:21)
And in the fifth year died Jehudith, the daughter of Beeri, the wife of Esau, in the land of Canaan, and she had no sons but daughters only.

(Jasher 30:22)
And these are the names of her daughters which she bore to Esau, the name of the elder was Marzith, and the name of the younger was Puith.

(Jasher 30:23)
And when Jehudith died, Esau rose up and went to Seir to hunt in the field, as usual, and Esau dwelt in the land of Seir for a long time.

(Jasher 30:24)
And in the sixth year Esau took for a wife, in addition to his other wives, Ahlibamah, the daughter of Zebeon the Hivite, and Esau brought her to the land of Canaan.

(Jasher 30:25)
And Ahlibamah conceived and bare to Esau three sons, Yeush, Yaalan, and Korah.

(Jasher 30:26)
And in those days, in the land of Canaan, there was a quarrel between the herdsmen of Esau and the herdsmen of the inhabitants of the land of Canaan, for Esau's cattle and goods were too abundant for him to remain in the land of Canaan, in his father's house, and the land of Canaan could not bear him on account of his cattle.

(Jasher 30:27)
And when Esau saw that his quarreling increased with the inhabitants of the land of Canaan, he rose up and took his wives and his sons and his daughters, and all belonging to him, and the cattle which he possessed, and all his property that he had acquired in the land of Canaan, and he went away from the inhabitants of the land to the land of Seir, and Esau and all belonging to him dwelt in the land of Seir.

(Jasher 30:28)
But from time to time Esau would go and see his father and mother in the land of Canaan, and Esau intermarried with the Horites, and he gave his daughters to the sons of Seir, the Horite.

(Jasher 30:29)
And he gave his elder daughter Marzith to Anah, the son of Zebeon, his wife's brother, and Puith he gave to Azar, the son of Bilhan the Horite; and Esau dwelt in the mountain, he and his children, and they were fruitful and multiplied.

(Genesis 29:21) (Jasher 31:1...) (Jubilees 28:2)

And in the seventh year, in the first year of the third week Jacob's service which he served Laban was completed. And Jacob said to Laban, Give me my wife, for whom I have served you seven years for my days of my service are fulfilled, that I may go in to her. And Laban said to Jacob: I will give you your wife.

(Genesis 29:22) (...Jasher 31:1) (Jubilees 28:3...)

And Laban did so, and Laban and Jacob gathered together all the men of the place, and made a feast.

(Genesis 29:23...) (Jasher 31:3)

And it came to pass in the evening, Laban came to the house, and afterward Jacob came there with the people of the feast, and Laban extinguished all the lights that were there in the house.

(Jasher 31:3)
And Jacob said to Laban, Why do you do this thing to us? And Laban answered, Such is our custom to act in this land.

(...Genesis 29:23...) (Jasher 31:4) (...Jubilees 28:3...)

And after that he took Leah his elder daughter, and brought her to Jacob and gave her to Jacob as a wife;

(Jasher 31:6)
And all the people at the feast knew what Laban had done to Jacob, but they did not tell the thing to Jacob.

(Jasher 31:7)
And all the neighbors came that night to Jacob's house, and they ate and drank and rejoiced, and played before Leah upon

timbrels, and with dances, and they responded before Jacob, Heleah, Heleah.

(Jasher 31:8)
And Jacob heard their words but did not understand their meaning, but he thought such might be their custom in this land.

(Jasher 31:9)
And the neighbors spoke these words before Jacob during the night, and all the lights that were in the house Laban had that night extinguished.

(...Genesis 29:23) (Jasher 31:4) (...Jubilees 28:3..., 4...)
And Jacob went in to her, and Jacob did not know that she was Leah, for he thought that she was Rachel.

(Genesis 29:24) (Jasher 31:5) (...Jubilees 28:3)
And Laban gave to his daughter Leah Zilpah his maid for a handmaid.

(Genesis 29:25...) (Jasher 31:10) (...Jubilees 28:4...)
And it came to pass, that in the morning, when daylight appeared, Jacob turned to his wife and he saw, and behold, it was Leah that had been lying in his bosom, and Jacob said, Behold now I know what the neighbors said last night, Heleah, they said, and I knew it not.

(...Genesis 29:25) (Jasher 31:11) (...Jubilees 28:4)
And Jacob was angry with Laban. And Jacob called to Laban and he said to Laban, What is this you have done to me? Did I not serve with you for Rachel and not for Leah? Why then have you beguiled me and gave me Leah?

(...Jubilees 28:5...)
Take your daughter, and I will go; for you have done evil to me.

(Genesis 29:26) (Jasher 31:12...) (Jubilees 28:6...)
And Laban answered Jacob and said to Jacob: It must not be so done in our country, to give the younger before the firstborn.

(...Jubilees 28:6)
And it is not right to do this; for thus it is ordained and written in the heavenly tablets, that no one should give his younger daughter before the elder; but the elder, one gives first and after her the younger - and the man who does so, they set down guilt against him in heaven, and none is righteous that does this thing, for this deed is evil before the Lord.

(Jubilees 28:7)
And command you the children of Israel that they do not this thing; let them neither take nor give the younger before they have given the elder, for it is very wicked.

(Genesis 29:27) (...Jasher 31:12) (Jubilees 28:8)
And Laban said to Jacob: Now therefore if you desire to take her sister likewise, fulfill her week. Let the seven days of the feast of this one pass by. And we will give you this also, I shall give you Rachel, Take her to you for the service which you shall serve with me yet seven other years, that you may pasture my sheep as you did in the former week.

(Genesis 29:28) (Jasher 31:13...) (Jubilees 28:9...)
And Jacob did so, and fulfilled her week. And on the day when the seven days of the feast of Leah had passed, he gave him Rachel his daughter to wife also, that he might serve him another seven years.

(Genesis 29:29) (...Jasher 31:13...) (Jubilees 28:10)

And Laban gave to Rachel his daughter Bilhah his handmaid, the sister of Zilpah, to be her maid.

(Genesis 29:30) (...Jasher 31:13) (...Jubilees 28:5, 10)

And he went in also to Rachel, and he loved also Rachel more than Leah, and served with him yet seven other years for Rachel, for Leah had been given to him for nothing.

(Genesis 29:31) (Jasher 31:14) (Jubilees 28:11..., 12)

And when the LORD saw that Leah was hated and Rachel loved, He opened her womb and she conceived and bare Jacob four sons in those days, but Rachel was barren.

(Genesis 29:32) (...Jubilees 28:11)

And Leah conceived, and bore Jacob a son, and she called his name Reuben: on the fourteenth day of the ninth month, in the first year of the third week, for she said, Surely the LORD has looked on my affliction; now therefore my husband will love me.

(Genesis 29:33) (Jubilees 28:13)

And again, Jacob went in to Leah, and she conceived again, and bore Jacob a second son and said, Because the LORD has heard that I was hated, he has therefore given me this son also: and she called his name Simeon on the twenty-first of the tenth month, and in the third year of this week.

(Genesis 29:34) (Jubilees 28:14)

And again, Jacob went in to Leah, and she conceived again, and bore him a third son; and said, Now, this time will my husband be joined to me, because I have born him three sons: therefore, his name was called Levi in the new moon of the first month in the sixth year of this week.

(Genesis 29:35...) (Jubilees 28:15)

And again, Jacob went in to her, and she conceived again, and bore him a fourth son and she said, Now I will praise the LORD: therefore she called his name Judah in the first year of the fourth week.

(...Genesis 29:35) (Jasher 31:15)

And these are their names, Reuben Simeon, Levi, and Judah, and she afterward left bearing.

Genesis: Chapter Thirty

(Genesis 30:1) (Jasher 31:16...) (Jubilees 28:16...)

And when Rachel was barren, and saw that she bore Jacob no children, Rachel envied her sister Leah, on account of all this; and said to Jacob, Give me children, or else I die.

(Genesis 30:2) (...Jubilees 28:16)

And Jacob's anger was kindled against Rachel: and he said, Am I in God's stead, who has withheld from you the fruit of the womb? Have I withheld from you the fruits of your womb? Have I forsaken you?

(Genesis 30:3) (...Jasher 31:16...) (Jubilees 28:17...)

And when Rachel saw that Leah had borne four sons to Jacob, Reuben and Simeon and Levi and Judah, she took her handmaid Bilhah, and she said, Behold my maid Bilhah, go in to her; and she shall conceive, and bear a son to me on my knees, that I may also have children by her.

(Genesis 30:4) (...Jubilees 28:17, 18...)

And she gave him Bilhah her handmaid to wife: and Jacob went in to her.

(Genesis 30:5) (Jasher 31:16...) (...Jubilees 28:18...)

And he went in to her, and Bilhah conceived, and bore Jacob a son.

(Genesis 30:6) (...Jasher 31:16...) (...Jubilees 28:18)

And Rachel said, God has judged me, and has also heard my voice, and has given me a son: therefore, she called his name

Dan on the ninth of the sixth month, in the sixth year of the third week.

(Genesis 30:7) (...Jasher 31:16...) (Jubilees 28:19...)
And Jacob went in again to Bilhah Rachel's maid a second time, and she conceived again, and bore Jacob a second son.

(Genesis 30:8) (...Jasher 31:16) (...Jubilees 28:19)
And Rachel said, With great wrestlings have I wrestled with my sister, and I have prevailed: and she called his name Naphtali on the fifth of the seventh month, in the second year of the fourth week.

(Genesis 30:9) (Jasher 31:17...) (Jubilees 28:20...)
When Leah saw that she had become sterile and that she had left bearing, she envied Rachel, she also took Zilpah her maid, and gave her Jacob to wife, and Jacob also came to Zilpah.

(Genesis 30:10) (Jasher 31:17...) (...Jubilees 28:20...)
And Zilpah Leah's maid conceived and bore Jacob a son.

(Genesis 30:11) (...Jasher 31:17...) (...Jubilees 28:20...)
And Leah said, A troop comes: and she called his name Gad on the twelfth of the eighth month, in the third year of the fourth week.

(Genesis 30:12) (...Jasher 31:17...) (Jubilees 28:21...)
And he went in again to her, and she conceived, and Zilpah Leah's maid bore Jacob a second son.

(Genesis 30:13) (...Jasher 31:17) (...Jubilees 28:21)
And Leah said, I am happy, for the daughters will call me blessed: and she called his name Asher on the second of the eleventh month, in the fifth year of the fourth week.

(Genesis 30:14)

And Reuben went in the days of wheat harvest, and found mandrakes in the field, and brought them to his mother Leah. Then Rachel said to Leah, Give me, I pray, of your son's mandrakes.

(Genesis 30:15)

And she said to her, Is it a small matter that you have taken my husband? And would you take away my son's mandrakes also? And Rachel said, Therefore, he shall lie with you to night for your son's mandrakes.

(Genesis 30:16)

And Jacob came out of the field in the evening, and Leah went out to meet him, and said, You must come in to me; for surely I have hired you with my son's mandrakes. And he lay with her that night.

(Genesis 30:17) (Jasher 31:18...) (Jubilees 28:22...)

And Jacob went in to Leah, and God hearkened to Leah, and she again conceived, and bore Jacob the fifth son.

(Genesis 30:18) (...Jasher 31:18...) (...Jubilees 28:22)

And Leah said, God has given me my hire, because I have given my maiden to my husband: and she called his name Issachar on the fourth of the fifth month, in the fourth year of the fourth week, and she gave him to a nurse.

(Genesis 30:19) (...Jasher 31:18...) (Jubilees 28:23...)

And Jacob went in again to Leah and she conceived again, and bore Jacob two children, the sixth son and a daughter.

(Genesis 30:20) (...Jasher 31:18...) (...Jubilees 28:23...)

And Leah said, God has endued me with a good dowry; now

will my husband dwell with me, because I have born him six sons: and she called his name Zebulun.

(Genesis 30:21) (...Jasher 31:18) (...Jubilees 28:23)
And afterwards she bore a daughter, their sister, and called her name Dinah in the seventh of the seventh month, in the sixth year of the fourth week.

(Jasher 31:19)
And Rachel was still barren in those days, and Rachel prayed to the Lord at that time, and she said, O Lord God remember me and visit me, I beseech you, for now my husband will cast me off, for I have borne him no children.

(Jasher 31:20)
Now O Lord God, hear my supplication before you, and see my affliction, and give me children like one of the handmaids, that I may no more bear my reproach.

(Genesis 30:22) (Jasher 31:21...) (Jubilees 28:24...)
And God remembered Rachel, and God hearkened to her. And the Lord was gracious to Rachel and opened her womb.

(Genesis 30:23) (...Jasher 31:21...) (...Jubilees 28:24...)
And she conceived, and bore a son; and said, The Lord God has taken away my reproach:

(Genesis 30:24) (...Jasher 31:21) (...Jubilees 28:24)
And she called his name Joseph on the new moon of the fourth month, in the sixth year in this fourth week. And said, The LORD shall add to me another son. And Jacob was ninety-one years old when she bore him.

(Jasher 31:22)
At that time Jacob's mother, Rebecca, sent her nurse Deborah the daughter of Uz, and two of Isaac's servants to Jacob.

(Jasher 31:23)
And they came to Jacob to Haran and they said to him, Rebecca has sent us to you that you shall return to your father's house to the land of Canaan; and Jacob hearkened to them in this which his mother had spoken.

(Genesis 30:25) (Jasher 31:24...) (Jubilees 28:25...)
At that time, the other seven years which Jacob served Laban for Rachel were completed, and it was at the end of fourteen years that he had dwelt in Haran. And it came to pass, when Rachel had born Joseph, that Jacob said to Laban, Send me away, that I may go to my own place, and to my country, for behold my mother sent to me from the land at Canaan that I should return to my father's house.

(Genesis 30:26) (...Jasher 31:24) (...Jubilees 28:25)
Give me my wives and my children, for whom I have served you, and let me go to my father Isaac, and let me make me a house: for you know my service which I have done you. I have completed the years in which I have served you for your two daughters, and I will go to the house of my father.

(Genesis 30:27) (Jasher 31:25...) (Jubilees 28:26)
And Laban said to him, Not so I pray, if I have found favor in your eyes, tarry with me for your wages, and pasture my flock for me again, and take your wages: for I have learned by experience that the LORD has blessed me for your sake.

(Genesis 30:28) (...Jasher 31:25)
And he said, Tell me your wages, and I will give it, and remain with me.

(Genesis 30:29)

And he said to him, You know how I have served you, and how your cattle was with me.

(Genesis 30:30)

For it was little which you had before I came, and it is now increased to a multitude; and the LORD has blessed you since my coming: and now when shall I provide for my own house also?

(Genesis 30:31) (Jasher 31:26...)

And he said, What shall I give you? And Jacob said to him, You shall not give me anything: if you will do this thing for me, I will again feed and keep your flock as at first:

(Genesis 30:32) (...Jasher 31:26)

I will pass through all your flock today, removing from there all the speckled and spotted cattle, and all the brown cattle among the sheep, and the spotted and speckled among the goats: and of such shall be my hire.

(Genesis 30:33)

So shall my righteousness answer for me in time to come, when it shall come for my hire before your face: every one that is not speckled and spotted among the goats, and brown among the sheep, that shall be counted stolen with me.

(Jubilees 28:27)

And they agreed with one another that he should give him as his wages those of the lambs and kids which were born black and spotted and white, these were to be his wages.

(Genesis 30:34)

And Laban said, Behold, I would it might be according to your word.

(Genesis 30:35) (Jasher 31:27, 28...)

And Laban did so, and Laban removed that day from his flock all that Jacob had said - the he goats that were ringstraked and spotted, and all the she goats that were speckled and spotted, and every one that had some white in it, and all the brown among the sheep - and gave them to Jacob. And Jacob placed all that he had removed from Laban's flock and gave them into the hand of his sons.

(Genesis 30:36) (...Jasher 31:28)

And he set three days' journey between himself and Jacob: and Jacob fed the rest of Laban's flocks.

(Jasher 31:29)
And when the servants of Isaac which he had sent to Jacob saw that Jacob would not then return with them to the land of Canaan to his father, they then went away from him, and they returned home to the land of Canaan.

(Jasher 31:30)
And Deborah remained with Jacob in Haran, and she did not return with the servants of Isaac to the land of Canaan, and Deborah resided with Jacob's wives and children in Haran.

(Genesis 30:37)

And Jacob took him rods of green poplar, and of the hazel and chestnut tree; and pilled white strakes in them, and made the white appear which was in the rods.

(Genesis 30:38)

And he set the rods which he had pilled before the flocks in the gutters in the watering troughs when the flocks came to drink, that they should conceive when they came to drink.

(Genesis 30:39) (Jubilees 28:28)

And the flocks conceived before the rods, and brought forth cattle ringstraked, speckled, and spotted and black, variously marked, and they brought forth again lambs like themselves, and all that were spotted were Jacob's and those which were not were Laban's.

(Genesis 30:40)

And Jacob separated the lambs, and set the faces of the flocks toward the ringstraked, and all the brown in the flock of Laban; and he put his own flocks by themselves, and put them not to Laban's cattle.

(Genesis 30:41)

And it came to pass, whenever the stronger cattle conceived, that Jacob laid the rods before the eyes of the cattle in the gutters, that they might conceive among the rods.

(Genesis 30:42)

But when the cattle were feeble, he put them not in: so the feebler were Laban's, and the stronger Jacob's.

(Jasher 31:31)
And Jacob served Laban six years longer, and when the sheep brought forth, Jacob removed from them such as were speckled and spotted, as he had determined with Laban, and Jacob did so at Laban's for six years, and the man increased abundantly and he had cattle and maid servants and men servants, camels, and donkeys.

(Jasher 31:32)
And Jacob had two hundred drove of cattle, and his cattle were of large size and of beautiful appearance and were very productive, and all the families of the sons of men desired to get some of the cattle of Jacob, for they were exceedingly prosperous.

(Jasher 31:33)
And many of the sons of men came to procure some of Jacob's flock, and Jacob gave them a sheep for a man servant or a maid servant or for an donkey or a camel, or whatever Jacob desired from them they gave him.

(Genesis 30:43) (Jubilees 28:29)
And the man increased exceedingly, and had much cattle, oxen and sheep, and maidservants, and men servants, and camels, and donkeys.

Final Notes

We hope your journey is enriched and you are blessed through the production of the **Ancient Texts and the Bible** series!

Minister 2 Others would like to hear from you. If you have comments or questions concerning our materials, or if you find errors in our projects, misspellings, or formatting issues. We work hard to provide quality materials, however, sometimes things can squeak by unnoticed. Your feedback is truly appreciated.

We love producing helpful, innovative books and we are grateful for your support! If you have enjoyed this production, please consider writing a review and letting others know about our materials.

If you would like to be updated when we release new books and other materials, please sign up for our e-newsletter on our website.

Thanks!

Minister 2 Others

Minister2others.com

www.ingramcontent.com/pod-product-compliance
Lightning Source LLC
Chambersburg PA
CBHW071302190726
48292CB00007B/2646

* 9 7 8 1 9 4 7 7 5 1 2 1 7 *